THE SOCIAL ATOM

THE
SOCIAL ATOM

Why the Rich Get Richer, Cheaters
Get Caught, and Your Neighbor
Usually Looks Like You

Mark Buchanan

BLOOMSBURY

Published by Bloomsbury USA, New York
Distributed to the trade by Holtzbrinck Publishers

All papers used by Bloomsbury USA are natural, recyclable products made
from wood grown in well-managed forests. The manufacturing processes
conform to the environmental regulations of the country of origin.

LIBRARY OF CONGRESS CATALOGING–IN–PUBLICATION DATA

Buchanan, Mark.
    The social atom : why the rich get richer, cheaters get caught, and your
neighbor usually looks like you / Mark Buchanan.
        p. cm.
    ISBN-13: 978-1-59691-013-3
    ISBN 10: 1-59691-013-5
    1. Collective behavior. 2. Segregation. 3. Ethnic relations. I. Title.

HM866.B83 2007
302.3'5—dc22

                                                    2007001088

First U.S. Edition 2007

1   3   5   7   9   10   8   6   4   2

Typeset by Westchester Book Group
Printed in the United States of America by Quebecor World Fairfield

CONTENTS

PREFACE

I N T H E E A R L Y 1970s, it seemed pretty obvious to most people that the stubborn persistence of racial segregation in New
York, Chicago, and other U.S. cities had a lot to do with racism.
Blacks were confined to inner-city enclaves of desperate poverty,
with whites in affluent surrounding suburbs. Studies had found
widespread racial bias on the part of businesses, in hiring, promo-
tion and pay, and in the real estate industry, which tried to keep
blacks out of white neighborhoods. The link between racism and
segregation seemed undeniable. Even so, an economist at Harvard University wondered if everyone might be overlooking a
less obvious but more important factor. Thomas Schelling wondered if racial segregation might, in principle, have absolutely
nothing to do with racism.

Schelling set out to explore his idea with an unusual
method—using a checkerboard and a handful of coins. The
squares on the checkerboard were meant to represent houses, and
the coins people—darker coins for blacks, lighter coins for
whites. On the grid, he first placed an equal number of black and
white coins, mixed at random, depicting a fully integrated society. Then he began moving the coins around to see how this society's makeup might change with time. The idea was to make

simple assumptions about the factors that might influence people's movements, then use the coins to see what this might lead to. In a first experiment, Schelling supposed that people, being racist, would move houses if they looked to their neighbors and found even one person from the "other" race. Considering each coin in turn, he used this rule to see if it should stay put or move to some open square nearby. Unsurprisingly, he found that the society segregated quickly, light and dark coins gathering together. Racism can cause segregation—no surprise there.

But if you see segregation, is it necessarily caused by racism? This is a different question, and to answer it, Schelling devised a second experiment. Now he supposed that everyone would be perfectly happy to live next door to members of the other race and made only one minor concession to the reality of human nature. Even racially tolerant people, he mused, might prefer to avoid being part of an *extreme* minority. A white man might have black friends and colleagues and be happy to live in a predominantly black neighborhood. Just the same, he might prefer not to be one of the *only* whites living there. This isn't what we ordinarily think of as a "racist" attitude. In this experiment, Schelling supposed that all people would stay where they were unless they looked around and found that they were part of an extreme minority of less than, say, 30 percent.

You might expect that with everyone being content with full racial integration, the initial mixing of black and white would persist. But Schelling found, to the contrary, that the coins again segregated into entirely distinct enclaves. Figure 1, from a modern computer version of this experiment, shows how a well-mixed society, on the left, turns naturally into a segregated society, on the right, even though no single individual would have wanted this.

Before   After

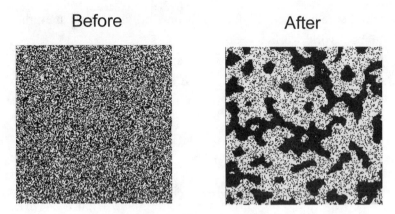

Figure 1

Paradoxically, people's innocent preference to avoid living in an extreme minority ends up obliterating mixed communities altogether. In a short paper in 1971, Schelling announced a bizarre conclusion—that even if every trace of racism were to vanish tomorrow, something akin to a law of physics might still make the races separate, much like oil and water.[1]

Schelling's segregation game is one of the all-time classics of social science. It obviously implies that anyone looking at racial segregation had better think long and hard before placing the blame solely upon racist attitudes. But it also holds a more general message. We tend to think that the behavior of a group or community should, in a fairly straightforward way, reflect the character of the people making it up. If a mob of people go crazy, rioting and smashing up storefronts, we usually seek an explanation in their individual anger and what caused it. This seems almost obvious, and yet Schelling's game implies that this idea is in fact a fallacy; that social outcomes needn't, at least in some cases, reflect in any obvious way the desires or intentions, habits or attitudes, of anyone at all. It suggests that something may be deeply out of kilter with our intuition about how the human world works.

But Schelling's work also offers a positive message—that a good way to get some insight into the human world is to step back from our usual fixation on the nuances of individual human psychology, and to follow a more simpleminded approach. We should think of people as if they were atoms or molecules following fairly simple rules and try to learn the patterns to which those rules lead. His implicit point is that seemingly complicated social happenings may often have quite simple origins, and that we can discover such simplicity by examining how we too may be subject to laws not unlike those of physics. This book is an exploration of that idea—and of a deep shift in science associated with it.

A few years ago, I worked as an editor for *Nature*, arguably the world's premier journal of science. I noticed then that the authors of some of the research papers landing on my desk were quite seriously seeking to find mathematical regularities in the human world of the kind we know from physics; in effect, they were trying to do social science along the lines of physics. In retrospect, I think I now recognize what was happening—after many years of neglect, researchers were finally beginning to take Schelling's way of thinking seriously.[2] Since then, an explosion of modern research in what I like to call "social physics" has convinced me that we stand at an important moment in history. We're now witnessing something akin to a "quantum revolution" in the social sciences. While we may be a long way from identifying strict "laws" for the human world, scientists have discovered lawlike regularities there and now recognize that such regularities in no way conflict with the existence of individual free will; we can be free individuals whose actions, in combination, lead to predictable outcomes for the collective. This is much as one finds in physics, where atomic-level chaos gives way to the clockwork precision of thermodynamics or planetary motion.

In pursuing social physics, researchers now also appreciate, as physicists have for many years, the magnificent power of the computer as a scientific tool. Through recorded history, the great philosophers and social theorists have played around with fascinating games of what-if. What if people are strictly greedy and selfish? Can society function, or will it finally collapse? What if people don't, when making decisions, always think for themselves, but simply imitate others? How does this alter social transformations? Unfortunately, these musings have largely remained sterile what-ifs because, with ten or a hundred people together, the growing web of causes and effects quickly overwhelms the power of even the greatest human mind to foresee what might come out. No more—or at least not always. Today, scientists have learned to augment the power of their minds with computing technology and, in "virtual" social experiments, are now routinely finding answers to what-if questions that probe the most fundamental social phenomena.

Without any pretense of completeness, rather with the aim of illustrating what I see as an exceptionally important way of thinking, I've tried to give here a sampling of some of the most exciting recent discoveries in this area of social physics. It seems to me that understanding collective organization and the laws of its evolution is clearly the key challenge of our age. From global warming and environmental degradation through to the renewed proliferation of nuclear weapons, mankind has never before faced such serious problems that stem so directly from our inability to manage our collective social activities. I don't believe that any great discovery of social physics will allow us to solve all these problems. If we do manage to steer a safe path into the future, for both humanity and the rest of the world, I imagine we'll do so by "muddling through," as we always have in the past. But our muddling skills will greatly be enhanced by a proper appreciation of the hidden forces that drive the world and that give shape and form to our collective lives.

Chapter 1

THINK PATTERNS, NOT PEOPLE

*To deride the hope of progress is the ultimate fatuity, the
last word in poverty of spirit and meanness of mind.*
—HENRY LOUIS MENCKEN

IT WAS THE summer of 1992, in a small sports hall in Split,
a city on the Dalmation coast of Croatia. Refugees from the
war in Bosnia were telling *Washington Post* journalist Peter
Maass what they had seen as eyewitnesses to the unbelievable,
to the overnight transformation of normal, decent human beings into remorseless killers. A farmer named Adem said that
Serbs from a neighboring village had rounded up thirty-five
men from his village and slit their throats. "They were killed,"
Maass reported, ". . . by Serbs who had been their friends, people who had helped harvest their fields the previous autumn,
people with whom they shared adolescent adventures and secrets, skinny-dipping in the Drina River on hot summer days,
groping with the naughty girls of the village at night. All of a
sudden, seemingly without reason, they had turned into
killers."[1]

In the early to mid 1990s, thousands of people like Adem, from Croatia, Bosnia, and Kosovo, told similar stories, of neighbors turning on neighbors and friends upon friends.

After the war, officials interviewed a man in Vukovar, a town in Croatia. "We all used to be friends," the man recalled of his Serbian and Bosnian Serb neighbors, "and we used to share happiness and sorrow with them." Then, in 1991, a poisonous cloud of hatred descended on the town. Greetings between neighbors, once expressions of lasting goodwill, evolved into crude displays of ethnic identification and solidarity, a way of telling "us" from "them." "You came to seek protection from people who until yesterday were your very good friends," the man recalled, "and who almost didn't recognize you anymore. They wouldn't dare to be your friends anymore."

What is terrifying and perplexing about events of this kind—alas, all too common in human history—is that they seem to turn up out of nowhere. One day all that appeared stable suddenly disintegrates, and people change beyond recognition, compelled by events to act in ways they would never before have dreamed of. It's as if mysterious forces suddenly take charge, and no one, even with the best of intentions, can stem the rolling tide of events.

In his book *Defying Hitler*, the German writer Sebastian Haffner recalls how he, an enemy of the Nazis, had been coerced into taking part in their activities. In the mid-1930s, when the Nazi army of intimidation, the brownshirts, marched through the streets, they beat anyone who failed to salute. Defiant in his own small way, Haffner often ducked into doorways. But when he and other students of law were ordered into an indoctrination camp, he found himself wearing a brown shirt and joining the very same marches. "Resistance would have been another form

of suicide," Haffner wrote, and the oppressed, unwittingly, became oppressor:

> When we came through villages, the people on either side of
> the road raised their arms to greet the flag, or disappeared
> quickly in some house entrance. They did this because they
> had learned that if they did not, we, that is I, would beat them
> up. It made not the slightest difference that I—and, no doubt
> others among us—ourselves fled into entryways to avoid these
> flags, when we were not marching behind them. Now we were
> the ones embodying an implicit threat of violence against all
> bystanders. They greeted the flag or disappeared. For fear of
> us. For fear of me . . .[2]

What makes completely ordinary and normal people plunge
headlong into collective madness? Is it even right to speak of
"madness" in referring to events such as those in Bosnia, or in
Nazi Germany, or in Rwanda in 1994, when extremist militias of
the ruling Hutu killed more than nine hundred thousand Tutsi
in less than a hundred days? Should we explain such events by
reference to the vagaries of human psychology and the moral
weakness of human nature? Or could there be a less mysterious,
if perhaps more alarming, cause?

In 1974, when the population of India topped 500 million, the
government under Indira Gandhi decided that it was time for extreme measures. "We have tried every trick in the book," the
health minister said at the time, "and now we have come to the
final chapter." He announced that "vasectomy camps" were being built around the country, and that, according to a new law,
men with three living children were to report to these camps to

be sterilized; those failing to "volunteer" would be arrested and taken by force. As a means of coercion, police withheld food rations cards, medical treatment, and driving licenses. In one village, they threatened to burn down the shop of a man unless he had a vasectomy, even though his wife was past childbearing age. In one year alone, more than 8 million people were sterilized.

Yet it soon became clear that Gandhi's government was battling against the social grain, driving individuals against their customs and beliefs, and against their own wishes. Amid violent protests, the government had to abandon the program—and India's population kept right on rising. India's population is still rising today—everywhere but in one exceptional province in the far south, Kerala, which is India's social miracle. Somehow, without brutality, coercion, or propaganda, Kerala has achieved what the rest of India has not.

Most Keralans are farmers and survive by growing rice, tea, or spices, such as cardamom and pepper. The typical Keralan owns little more than a few cooking utensils and tools, and earns seventy times less than the average American. Yet Keralans live to about seventy-two years on average, close to the U.S. average of about seventy-seven, and while elsewhere in India the population is surging, here it is stable. It's baffling. Economically and socially, Kerala looks much like the rest of rural India; it is no richer, its land no better. How can it be so different?

The one thing that makes Kerala different is education. Not education about birth control and family planning, as you might expect, but general education, in reading, writing, and arithmetic, and especially for women. In the late 1980s, the Keralan government—aided by volunteer organizations—undertook a massive effort to stamp out illiteracy in Kerala once and for all. Literally tens of thousands of volunteers crisscrossed the countryside and managed to track down over 150,000 illiterates, of whom two thirds were women. A small army of volunteer teachers then set to teaching them the basics. "Classes were held in cowsheds, in the open air, in courtyards," one leader of the effort told the *New York Times.*

Three years later, in 1991, the United Nations declared Kerala the world's only 100 percent literate state. And this remarkable achievement seems to have had a profound influence on population growth. As an Indian family-planning specialist noted in 1999, "People are now embarrassed to say if they have more than two kids . . . Seven or eight years ago, the norm was three children and we thought we were doing pretty good. Now it's two, and among the most educated people, it's one."

Economists and social researchers now agree that in Kerala, women's education is the magic bullet that has taken the air out of the great balloon of population growth—a balloon that had been ascending steadily for thousands of years. But how? Education has worked where programs of birth control and family planning, even forced sterilization, have failed. How does getting women to read newspapers and write diaries, to count past a hundred and multiply three-digit numbers, make such a difference?

THINKING IN PATTERNS

The central idea of this book is that the only way to understand a sudden explosion of ethnic nationalism, a peculiar link between women's education and birth control, entrenched racial segregation, and a host of other important or just plain interesting social phenomena—in financial markets, in politics, in the world of fashion—is to think of patterns, not people. There's an old way of thinking that says the social world is complicated because people are complicated. That's why, many people think, we've never been able to understand the human world with theories as reliable as those of physics and chemistry. Atoms are simple, people aren't, end of story. I hope to explain why this way of thinking is very much mistaken. People are sometimes complicated and hard to understand, but that's not the problem.

Anyone of driving age has had the irritating experience of cruising along the highway when suddenly the traffic grinds to a halt for no apparent reason. You creep along for thirty minutes, cursing the "idiots" in front of you, and straining to find something that might have made it happen. Yet there is no accident, no broken-down car, no workers doing road repairs. Then, just as abruptly, you come through it and traffic takes off again. Traffic experts call this a phantom jam, and it is a basic pattern that can arise, all on its own, on any roadway with too much traffic. Drivers can respond only so quickly to events around them, and as a road gets more crowded and the distance between cars shrinks, there comes a point when our reflexes can no longer cope. Any accidental clumping of cars tends to slow itself down, and so gather in more cars, making it go slower still and to gather in still more. A traffic jam emerges—automatically.

Go to a public square during a big protest or concert and you'll see something apparently very different, yet conceptually quite similar. If you watch closely, you'll see that how people move through a densely packed square really has less to do with individual inclinations than with patterns. As individuals try to avoid collisions with each other, as one person follows another, who in turn follows someone else, they automatically begin to form coherent streams of movement. To your immediate left and right others move in your direction, while farther away they go in other directions. A person has good reason to move within these streams, as moving in other directions is a lot more difficult. Because of this advantage, any stream soon attracts more people to join it, making it bigger and still more attractive to others. The pattern constrains people's choices, making them more likely to act in a way that reinforces the pattern, boosting its energy and influence.

These examples illustrate, in simple situations, the bizarre and convoluted link between individual desires and social outcomes. No one ever wants to start a traffic jam. For the phantom jams that plague roads all over the world every day, you cannot even point to any driver whose bad behavior made it happen. Likewise, no single person in a crowd starts out to create streams of movement or plots out where they should go. The patterns arise spontaneously out of the tumult and confusion and take on energy and power all their own. It is like choreography, yet without a choreographer. Where people go, along circuitous, snakelike paths, may well not reflect the actual desires of any single person or even an average of them all.

In 2004, Americans were stunned by photos showing the sadistic torture and humiliation of Iraqi prisoners by American soldiers at the Abu Ghraib prison in Baghdad. It seemed beyond belief that men and women of the U.S. military, ordinary kids who went to ordinary high schools and colleges across the country, could have taken part with apparent joy in the ritual humiliation and beating of defenseless prisoners. Yet a plausible explanation is actually not so hard to find—and it has a lot to do with bad patterns, rather than bad people. Three decades ago, psychologist Philip Zimbardo and colleagues at Stanford University took ordinary college students and, in an experiment, put them into a prisonlike setting in the basement of the psychology department. Some were to play prisoners, and others guards. The researchers took away the students' ordinary clothes, gave them uniforms and numbers; the guards were given silver reflecting sunglasses and generic names such as Mr. Correctional Officer. The psychologists' aim was to strip away the veneer of the students' individuality and to see what the situation might produce on its own. This is Zimbardo's description of what happened:

> Every day the level of hostility, abuse, and degradation of the prisoners became worse and worse and worse. Within 36 hours the first prisoner had an emotional breakdown, crying, screaming, and thinking irrationally. We had to release him, and each day after that we had to release another prisoner because of extreme stress reactions. The study was supposed to run for two weeks, but I ended it after six days because it was literally out of control. Kids we chose because they were normal and healthy were breaking down. Kids who were pacifists were acting sadistically, taking pleasure in inflicting cruel, evil punishment on prisoners.

Zimbardo has recently argued that what happened at Abu Ghraib followed the same pattern; it had to do not so much with the individuals, as with the situation they were in.[3] In many of the pictures, the soldiers weren't wearing their uniforms; psychologically, they were anonymous and "de-individuated" as "prison guards." Dehumanizing labels such as "detainees" or "terrorists" distinguished the prisoners as inferior and worthless, and there was confusion about responsibility and little supervision of the prison at night. This may not be a recipe that guarantees abuse, in all circumstances, but it certainly sets up the conditions by which it might grow and feed on itself. The more soldiers mistreated the prisoners, the more they saw them as less than human and even more worthy of that abuse.

Now think again of what happened in the former Yugoslavia, or the way mere education brought the growth of Kerala's population under control. Think about patterns, and not just people, and you can begin to see that these events, and others like them, needn't seem so inexplicable. As we will explore in detail later on, ethnic hatred and distrust can feed on itself. Indeed, it appears that the basic logic of human cooperation, in the midst of primitive social and economic conditions, even ensures in some cases that the blind distrust of people who are superficially different— culturally, religiously, or in other terms—offers an effective way for communities to build their own cohesiveness, however evil and destructive it may appear from outside. Simple mathematical analysis, as we'll see, suggests that the terrible pattern of ethnocentrism has a self-propelling energy of its own that many individuals simply cannot resist. Or think of education in Kerala. As women have become educated in Western nations over the past fifty years, birthrates have gradually fallen. This in itself is no great mystery, as education empowers women to seek other interests outside the home, in employment or otherwise. What seems so bizarre in the case of Kerala's example is the suddenness of the transition. But the secret to understanding, again, seems to lie in a pattern that has reinforced itself. No person lives in isolation, unaffected by the actions of others. When everyone else is educated, and when life comes to depend on education, then what was formerly an understandable decision to forgo education now becomes obviously unattractive to everyone. Education itself becomes self-sustaining, not because people have changed as individuals, not because of human psychology, but because of the logic of collective patterns and what supports them.

I think all of us have an intuition for this kind of thing—for the way our actions as individuals feed into the social world around us and help to create a reality that then acts back on us, pushing us one way or another, with consequences that may be good or bad. We get drawn into social streams and, in so doing, make them even more powerful and persuasive for the next person. Without intending to, we help create fashions and youth movements, waves of hysteria, religious cults, nationalistic fervor, or stock market euphoria. It seems likely that we often ride along on the energy of hidden social streams without even noticing their existence, while they influence the way we think, make us align ourselves with some ideas rather than others, or affect what we find fashionable and socially acceptable.

But there is another way to look at all this—it follows a close analogy with physics.

THE SOCIAL ATOM

A lot of what physicists have done over the past century and are still doing today aims at understanding what happens when lots of atoms interact with one another. Depending on the kinds of atoms, and especially on how they go together, the pattern of their mingling, you get such things as liquids and solids, metals that conduct electricity or rubber that doesn't, semiconductors and superconductors and liquid crystals and magnets. The most important lesson of modern physics is that it is often not the properties of the parts that matter most, but their organization, their pattern and form. That's true at the level of atoms and molecules, and well above that level too. Although we often fail to take note, much of what we see in the world is due to pattern and organization.

If you walk on the frozen tundra on the Norwegian island of Spitsbergen, part of the Svalbard chain and located six hundred

Figure 2

miles from the north pole, you will see what look like the signs of ancient human activity. The soil is stony, and in some places the stones have been piled up carefully and precisely into circular, ringlike mounds roughly six feet across (see figure 2). This geometric perfection seems to have been created with care and patience—but by whom, and for what purpose? Scientists now know, in fact, that there is no purpose; the pattern has emerged quite on its own by the action of natural, if somewhat hidden, forces. As geophysicists Brad Werner and Mark Kessler demonstrated a couple of years ago, the basic driving force is simply the cycle of freezing and thawing.

Here's what happens. Suppose, to begin with, that there were no rings, but that the mixture of soil and stones wasn't absolutely uniform; that just by accident you have more stones in some places, and more soil in others. Whenever the temperature drops below freezing—which happens frequently here—areas with more stones freeze slightly faster than those with less. That's because soil contains more water, and so places with more soil freeze more slowly. This slight imbalance in the freezing rate creates what geophysicists call frost heave—forces of expansion that push the soil toward soil-rich areas and the stones toward stonier places. Automatically, as if by magic, a natural sorting process separates the soil from the stones, pushing them to different places. Consequently, the initially random variations in soil and stone will be amplified, leading to regions of mostly soil and others of mostly stone.

But this is only half the story—then something else happens. As the stones gather in piles, they get heaped up higher and higher. But heaps that get too high become unstable, and avalanches then move some of the stones downhill, which makes the heaps spread into long ridges that gradually grow longer. In some cases, these ridges of stones grow until they decorate entire hillsides, while in others their ends eventually join to form squares or triangles, which then evolve into circles, as in figure 2 (taken in Spitsbergen by Mark Kessler). Computer simulations of the basic process of self-organization show that this explanation accounts perfectly for the size and layout of the real-world patterns. There is no need for human "intelligence" or activity at all.[4]

Over the past few decades, scientists and engineers have found similar "self-organization" at work in literally thousands of settings—in the biological chemistry that puts stripes on a tiger's back or a butterfly's wing, in waves on the sea, sand dunes in the desert, or the great cyclonic wind patterns of hurricanes. The essence of self-organization is that a pattern—a ring of stones or the precise arrangement of atoms in a crystal—emerges on its own and in a way that has little or nothing to do with the detailed properties of the parts making it up. No study of the soil or stones of Spitsbergen would ever explain the perfectly circular patterns, just as no study of air molecules on their own could help anyone understand a hurricane. The explanation requires thinking at the level of pattern and organization and form rather than of atoms or microscopic parts of any kind.

What about people? It is obvious, or should be obvious, that we're probably subject to the same kinds of processes of collective organization. Thomas Schelling's explanation of persisting segregation offers a clear enough example. If we think of people as the "atoms" or elementary building blocks of the social world, the "social atoms," then we might well expect large-scale patterns to emerge at the level of groups that have little to do with the character of the people themselves. Maybe communities, government institutions, markets, and social classes could be something like stone ridges—structures that no one "called for" but that organized themselves following inevitable laws that we do not yet understand. Of course, we know this is true. Social scientists talk about some communities being more "cohesive" than others, and therefore better able to organize and respond to challenges. Management theorists insist that some companies are more adaptable and resilient than others, and that this has more to do with "organization" than with their better employees. Free market economists routinely invoke the magic of market self-organization, the Invisible Hand of Adam Smith, or what the Austrian economist Friedrich von Hayek called "spontaneous order"—the process by which the actions of individuals pursuing their own interests keeps the shelves of supermarkets full and produces most of those things that people need, without any kind of top-down control or central planning.

Even though people are a lot more complicated than atoms or stones, I hope it's clear that the basic project of social science does really seem a lot like physics. First you have to understand the character of the social atoms, then learn what happens when many such atoms interact, creating a rich world of collective patterns and outcomes. Encouragingly, this is precisely what some of the most exciting scientific work is beginning to do.

By No One's Intention

The essence of self-organization is that some thing or process A leads to another, B, which in turn leads to more of A, triggering more B, more A, and so on in an increasing spiral of feedback. The falling price of a stock makes people sell, thereby driving the price lower still. One person rioting attracts others to join in. A faint trail in a public park entices some people to take it, and their footsteps over the grass then make for a more visible trail that attracts others. Feedback is often crucially important, yet only comes into view when you think about the interactions among the various parts of some system, rather than focusing too narrowly on the parts themselves.

A few years ago, German physicist Dirk Helbing, inspired by Schelling's way of thinking, devised a simple model to explore the spontaneous formation of human "streams"—the way people group together and follow one another through crowds. People on foot generally try to go where they want, while not running into others. But this obvious fact, Helbing found, has some not-so-obvious consequences. He used the computer to simulate the movements of hundreds of "people" moving in opposite directions (say, left and right) along a wide hallway or sidewalk. Whenever necessary, these people would avoid collisions with others by shifting sideways a little, in one direction or the other. The simulations show that this simple individual behavior quickly leads to an organized flow and the formation of coherent lanes. Why? The secret is that when people shift sideways to avoid a collision, they move only as far as required to find others going in their same direction. This brings people of similar movement together. Naturally, any lane that forms—even momentarily and by accident—will tend to grow as other people join it. Lanes are the natural outcome in a crowd of moving people, structures that self-organize on their own, without human intention, just like the stone rings in Spitsbergen.[5]

Of course, self-organization is not always beneficial. In the early 1980s, transit authorities in Budapest, Hungary, often had several buses running on the same route during peak hours to handle the crowds. But they began getting complaints from passengers who were waiting for thirty to forty-five minutes for a bus, only to then have three buses arrive all at once. For the public, this was obviously due to the stupidity of the bus drivers, or maybe even some actively perverse policy of management. Fortunately, the city authorities were soon able to identify the real source of the problem, and thereby find a solution as well. As it turns out, if you set three or more buses on a route, spacing them out equally, they won't stay that way. A bus running behind another bus tends to pick up fewer people, on average, because the leading bus has already taken some away. So the second bus stops for a shorter time. Consequently, the second bus inevitably catches up to the first, and the third catches the second—everyone ends in a line through self-organization.

But this understanding also suggests a solution. The bus authorities recognized that the problem ultimately originates in that buses on the same route were never allowed to pass one another. This meant that those behind caught up to those ahead, but were never slipping past. To defuse the problem, the authorities instructed drivers to follow new rules: if they saw another bus on the same route stopped, even if it couldn't possibly pick up all the waiting passengers, they were to simply pass by and continue on. This broke up the natural clustering of buses, leading to more efficient transportation (although I'm sure it didn't please passengers who saw empty buses hurtling past).

Another example, also explored by Helbing and his colleagues, demonstrates how understanding social self-organization can make a huge difference in managing group behavior. They've adapted their model of pedestrians to explore how people behave in a panic situation—when trying to escape from a smoke-filled theater, for example. The simulations, on the one hand, demonstrate a lesson we all learned in childhood, which is "Don't run." A crowd rushing to the exit piles up in a traffic jam, whereas people avoid the jam and get out if they move more slowly. As Helbing puts it, "Slower is faster." But now for a bigger surprise. A room might obviously have some tables in it. How would their placement and size affect the escape of a crowd? It seems obvious that obstacles have to make the situation even worse. Yet, counterintuitively, they can sometimes be beneficial. In particular, a table placed a few feet in front of the exit can help regulate the human flow. The table changes the pattern of self-organization, helping everyone to get out more quickly.[6]

Learning how self-organization works—and how to manage it for human benefit—ought to be one of the main tasks of social science. Most people would, I think, see this as a plausible way for social scientists to approach their work. What is surprising, and more than a little puzzling, is that until recently, Schelling, Helbing, and a few other pioneers have been the exceptions—by tradition, few social researchers have actually worked this way.

A Peculiar Science

You'd expect that social scientists would spend time studying basic social phenomena—the formation of social classes, or the way the "culture" of a community or business firm can persist even as many people come and go. To explain them they would look to the basic features of human behavior—our tendency to copy others and fit in with those around us, or our ability to adapt rapidly to a changing world. The social world is made of people and arises out of the actions of people, so it should be explained by looking at people and how they interact with one another.

But many social scientists don't really work this way. Many researchers carry out surveys and look for "correlations" between one thing and another—poverty and crime rates, for example, or education and income. Finding a link, they say the one thing "explains" the other. Why is inner-city crime so high? Simple, it's because inner-city poverty is high, and the two things go together. There is nothing wrong with this, as the existence of a correlation or pattern that links two kinds of happenings indeed suggests that *something* interesting is going on. But inquiry often stops here, without exploring in detail how the actions of people may bring about the pattern; without seeking to bring the basic causal mechanism into view. How does poverty alter individual behavior? Why does this lead to crime? These kinds of questions go unexplored, as if social science were a branch of applied statistics.

Economists have another way of doing social science—today it is the dominant way—and it does focus on causes, on people and their motivations, and how these lead to social outcomes. But much of this work also has a peculiar quality to it. Some of the greatest economists—such as Milton Friedman in the

1950s—argued that theorists shouldn't bother trying to portray
a realistic picture of how individual people behave. Rather, they
should work with whatever picture they might find convenient
in building theories that let them make "predictions." The most
common assumptions are that people are perfectly rational and
infallible in their decision making, and ruthlessly greedy in pursuing their selfish ends. This approach still gravely afflicts the
profession, as does another—that the character of a group just reflects the character of the typical people who make it up. As I'll
explore in a little more detail later, economic theorists also generally assume—not in the pursuit of accuracy or reality, but to
keep their mathematics simple—that the actions of one person
never influence those of another.

Many other social scientists seem to have raised the flag of
permanent defeat and busy themselves with rehashing the works
of great thinkers of the past. There's no end to ongoing argument about what Hobbes or Weber or Durkheim or Smith actually meant to say, as opposed to what they seem to have said, or
what someone said they said.[7] And then finally, there is the lu-
natic fringe of those social scientists who seem to prefer a
"grand" style of thinking that rises up above the messy details of
the real world and takes flight in abstract theories, unrestricted by
any need to test those theories against reality. Nowhere is this
more evident than in the perversely influential "postmodernist"
school of thought, which insists that there isn't actually a real
world "out there" with objective properties that we can try
to understand. Instead, truth is completely arbitrary and "constructed" in a social manner by tacit agreement. Another common assertion is that because our thinking and communication
are so intimately linked with language, everything can be viewed
as a text, and social theory becomes more or less equivalent with

literary criticism. Nothing that anyone has ever written has a fixed or true meaning; readers make up the meaning as they go.

The British historian Geoffrey Elton referred to the postmodernist trend as "the intellectual equivalent of crack" for its seductive, anything-goes style of theorizing that essentially frees the author from any responsibility to think coherently.[8]

It seems to me that social science has ended up in a pretty weird place. But I also think that these kinds of social science are, fortunately, fast becoming relics of history, for two reasons. First, an outpouring of outstanding experimental work in psychology, over several decades, has shown that a lot of human behavior isn't nearly as complicated and hard to fathom as we've been led to believe. The "social atom," if you will, often follows fairly simple rules. Second, scientists are learning that what makes the social world complex isn't individual complexity, but the way the people go together, in often surprising ways, to create patterns.

In pursuing the idea that pattern is more important than people, we'll try to pin down the logic of the New York Stock Exchange, and other financial markets, to see how streams of thinking feed on themselves to create rallies and crashes that no one ever intended. We'll look at the curious and almost mechanical workings of rumors, fashions, and waves of hysteria—and see that our collective behavior follows mathematical patterns of surprising precision. We'll look at what happened in the former Yugoslavia, and in Rwanda, to draw out the hidden logic that drives ethnocentrism, and also travel back into the depths of our evolutionary history to see how the perpetual battle of one group against another, played out on the African savanna, has left its indelible mark on our most fundamental social habits—especially our ability to cooperate with or come to the aid of complete strangers.

Along the way, we'll also see how viewing people as the atoms of a social "substance" can help to explain many patterns that arise again and again in all human societies—the existence of social classes, for example, and the inexorable flow of wealth into the hands of the few. Today's researchers increasingly see the project of understanding the human social world as being akin to the effort, in physics, of understanding how atoms go together to make all the substances we know—some sticky, others slippery, some that conduct electricity, and others that don't. Diamonds don't glitter because the atoms making them up glitter, but because of the way those atoms fall together into a special pattern. It's often not the parts but the pattern that is most important, and so it is with people.

This book is about wealth, power and politics, class hatred, and racial segregation. It is about fads, fashions, and riots, spontaneous outbreaks of goodwill and trust within communities, and moods of dejection or buoyancy that sweep over financial markets. Mostly, it is about social surprises—events and changes that rise up out of nowhere to alter our lives—and why we seem so inept at perceiving their causes.

Chapter 2

THE "HUMAN" PROBLEM

Politics is the accomplishment of what would have happened anyway.

—HANS MAGNUS ENZENSBERGER

I N 1984, WILLIAM STERN had rather a lot on his plate— responsibility for nothing less than the revival of New York's famous Times Square, then a seedy netherworld of human squalor and sleaze. A native New Yorker and head of the Urban Development Corporation—a New York State organization charged with improving run-down urban locations—Stern had warm childhood memories of the square in another era. "In the early fifties," he recalls, "it had been a childhood delight for me. On Saturday, my father and I would bus down from Harlem to see a movie, often a Roy Rogers or Gene Autry cowboy picture. Then we'd get something to eat at Nedick's and afterward just stroll around, gazing up at the giant signs." But now everything was different: "I would walk through Times Square at night . . . a state trooper by my side, and feel revulsion. We'd hurry past prostitute-filled single-room-occupancy hotels and massage parlors, greasy spoons and pornographic bookstores; past X-rated

movie houses and peep shows and a pathetic assortment of
junkies and pushers and johns and hookers and pimps—the whole
panorama of big-city lowlife."[1]

During three decades of slow decay, virtually all "legitimate"
businesses had been driven from the area, which had become a
magnet for crime. In 1984 alone, police recorded more than two
thousand crimes in the single block along Forty-second Street
between Seventh and Eighth avenues—known as the "worst
block" in the city—and more than one in five of those were violent rapes or murders. Once the visual icon of the city, Times
Square now represented the fringe between civilization and
lawlessness.

But Stern and his team had a plan to change all that. Their
imaginative 42nd Street Redevelopment Plan aimed to spend
$2.6 billion in a strategic effort to restore Times Square to its for-
mer glory. They would build new office towers, hotels, and a
huge computer and garment wholesale mart covering several
blocks. They would restore historic old theaters—especially the
famous New Amsterdam—and renovate the dingy Forty-second
Street subway station. It was a grand strategy. But it fell to pieces
before even getting started. After the New York City Board of
Estimate finally approved the project in November of 1984, political squabbles watered down some of the boldest ideas. Then,
in October of 1987, the stock market crashed—falling a spectacular 22 percent in just one day. The financial shock knocked the
wind out of the commercial real estate market, and one by one,
law firms, advertisers, and banks—the major prospective tenants
for the project—pulled out. "Almost nothing we planned,"
Stern recalls, "ever came to fruition."

And so Stern's beloved Times Square was left to the indiffer-
ent forces of social nature—to drug dealers and pimps, to the

desperate, the addicted, and the abused. Then something funny happened: Times Square came surging back to life all on its own.

In 1990, entertainment giant Viacom signed a lease to occupy 1515 Broadway Avenue, the site of the old Astor Hotel. Two years later, international publisher Bertelsmann AG and investment bank Morgan Stanley also bought buildings on Broadway, and then in 1993, the Walt Disney Company agreed with the city to renovate the New Amsterdam Theatre. Once Disney came in, investment interest skyrocketed. Within the next few years, luxury hotels and office buildings popped up like dandelions; Madame Tussaud's Wax Museum opened a New York branch. The sex shops and strip clubs disappeared, and crime dropped to the point of being unnoticeable. By the late 1990s, Times Square was transformed and transfigured—the sleaze miraculously replaced by glass towers and shiny steel.

What made it happen? Stern readily admits the success had nothing to do with New York's building policy; he sees another explanation. "It had everything," he says, "to do with government policy that, by fighting crime, cracking down on the sex industry, and cutting taxes—albeit only selectively—at last allowed the market to do its work and bring the area back to life." The police started making arrests for minor crimes—their famous "zero tolerance" approach—and the city passed ordinances against the sex industry. These steps, Stern suggests, led directly to the revival of the area, and an outcome that teaches us a lesson: "There's a right way and a wrong way for government to pursue economic development."

Stern's explanation seems plausible. He watched the transformation as it was taking place and probably has as much chance as anyone of getting it right. But how do we know if he is right—or wrong? Is it even possible to know the "real truth" about Times

Square's revival? This may seem like an odd question, as there must certainly be a "real truth" about what happened. But if there is, going about finding it is far from easy. The difficulty points to a profound difference between the way we explain events in the human world, and how science explains events in the nonhuman world, mostly through the discovery of patterns and natural laws.

THE SCIENTIFIC RECIPE

During his most productive years, Danish astronomer Tycho Brahe didn't have much of a nose, most of it having been lopped off in 1566 by the sharp sword of Danish nobleman Manderup Parsberg, apparently after an argument over their relative skills in mathematics. Aged nineteen, Brahe had a nose-plate fashioned out of gold and silver, which served him nicely until he died in 1601—according to one story, after he unwisely held his bladder too long out of politeness at an important dinner.[2] The wine flowed, and Brahe couldn't bring himself to leave the table. After he left the party, as a biographer wrote in 1654, "hard pains followed and for five days, he could not sleep. Thereafter he could let out small amounts of urine, and fell into an uneasy sleep." Brahe died ten days later.

Aside from its tragic aspects, Brahe's life was marked by other assorted eccentricities—he kept a pet moose who drank beer and followed him around his castle on the island of Hven, between Denmark and Sweden. Yet Brahe's life wasn't one of rich indolence—his heroic scientific persistence helped establish a model for how good science is done. Every morning and night, for several decades, Brahe retired to a small observatory and—using his own handmade instruments—recorded the positions of the planet Mars, a tiny reddish pinprick of light sometimes

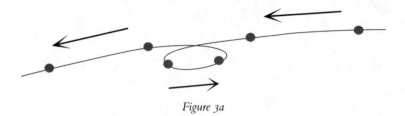

Figure 3a

visible on the horizon. In these days—before the telescope—astronomers had little idea of what the planets really were. What they did know was that the motion of Mars across the sky was by no means simple. Its position, noted at the same time each day, drifted gradually from west to east. But every two years, roughly, the planet would take a brief diversion, slowing down, going backward a little, and maybe doing a loop (see figure 3a), before apparently regaining its senses and continuing its normal motion.

In Brahe's time, no one could explain what was going on. But after he died in 1601, German astronomer Johannes Kepler was able to study the numbers in Brahe's notebooks and—after eight long years—found a hidden simplicity. Kepler discovered that all the strange numbers in Brahe's books, reflecting the seemingly crazy wanderings of Mars, weren't so strange after all. Both Mars and Earth, Kepler's mathematics revealed, were moving on simple elliptical paths around the Sun, with Earth on the inside track. Most of the time, when Earth isn't too close to Mars, this makes Mars, as seen from Earth, drift from west to east (as Earth moves from position 1 through position 3 in figure 3b). But because Earth completes each orbit faster than Mars (about twice as fast), Earth catches up to Mars and makes a close pass by every two years. As we pass by, over several months, Mars seems instead to drift east to west (as Earth moves from position 4 through position 5 in figure 3b).[3] Kepler was the first man ever

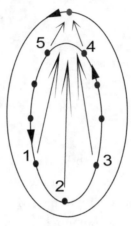

Figure 3b

to look to the sky with understanding—because he knew the pattern. Kepler's discovery, in turn, inspired Isaac Newton to find an explanation for this remarkable simplicity—the mathematical laws of gravity and motion.

Together, the trio of Brahe, Kepler, and Newton demonstrated a kind of recipe for good science—gather data, identify patterns, then find a mechanism to explain them. Patterns reveal regularities that show how the seemingly complicated actually isn't so. The natural laws behind those patterns often then lead to the possibility of prediction. Knowing the patterns of fluid dynamics, today's physicists and engineers can run computer simulations of aircraft behavior with immense confidence in their results. Aircraft manufacturers such as Boeing don't even need to test-fly their aircraft anymore. As a Boeing executive told me a few years ago, they only do test flights to reassure the public, who find it difficult to believe that science can be so capable. The patterns of quantum theory and relativity allow physicists to make predictions of truly astounding accuracy. Modern predictions of the magnetic strength of the electron, known as its magnetic moment, agree with the measured value to one part in 100 million[4]—an accuracy equivalent to firing a needle from ten miles and splitting a human hair.

Scientific laws often look like recipes; given ingredients A and B, you can be sure the result will be outcome C. Hydrogen mixed with oxygen leads, after a reaction, to water. Once you understand the law, you can apply it over and over. Newton's laws explain the motion of Mars, a telecommunications satellite, or a comet just as they do a baseball's curving trajectory toward home plate. Obviously, if we had a similar understanding of what we might call the "laws of redevelopment," we could look at Times Square and explain what happened quite easily. In the early 1990s, an explanation might go, the government wisely put conditions A and B in place, and the outcome—according to Stern's Law of Redevelopment—was the predictable C: steel buildings, wealth, and bright lights. Of course, no one is even remotely close to being able to do this.

Let's consider some of the alternatives to Stern's explanation. Perhaps, the revival was an accident. A few key investors coincidentally came into Times Square around the same time, and their activities then encouraged others. Or, one might note that Times Square has, historically, had many ups and downs. Maybe there's a natural cycle. The pendulum swings one way—property becomes cheap—and this sets the stage for a swing in the other direction. Depending on your personal experiences and philosophy, you might like one of these explanations. Or you might instead choose an alternative I haven't mentioned. But it is hard to deny that all of these hypothetical explanations lack authority because they're explanations after the fact. No one *predicted* the revival of Times Square. Similarly, there is no powerful theory that predicts

changes in crime rates, outbreaks of mass paranoia, the unexpected fates of governments. We cannot predict accurately what
will happen next month or even tomorrow in the stock market
(although many people make a comfortable living by convincing
others that they can).

"The aims of scientific thought," as the British philosopher
Alfred North Whitehead wrote, "are to see the general in the
particular and the eternal in the transitory." Unfortunately, when
it comes to human events, finding patterns, and especially finding
natural laws behind them, seems hard, if not impossible. Instead,
explanations usually rest on arguments and plausible stories, such
as Stern's. One might say that human science is largely "storytelling" science, based on the linking together of one event with
another.[5] We tell stories because we like stories—rich in detail,
drama, and unexpected twists, which capture the excitement and
tension of real life—but also because we lack an understanding
of scientific laws for the human world.

Even so, people are made of atoms and molecules. We're a
part of nature. If nature follows patterns that flow out of natural
laws, shouldn't we? One hundred fifty years ago, a man named
Henry Thomas Buckle certainly thought so.

IRRATIONAL EXUBERANCE

Halfway through the nineteenth century, Buckle—the son of a
wealthy English shipping magnate, and then twenty years old—
was the best chess player in Europe. Bored, apparently, he
abruptly gave up chess and turned his attention to world
history—setting out to write a work that would finally make the
study of man truly scientific. Perhaps no one has ever had such
confidence that a real science of man should be possible.

Buckle was clearly a product of his times. After Kepler and
Newton, scientists were laying bare the workings of the physical
world, with immense practical consequences—the steam engine
and the industrial revolution. Science seemed unstoppable. Indeed, Buckle noted that science doesn't have a reverse gear, but
spreads continuously and irreversibly. In the past, what has seemed
mysterious has ultimately been explained, and we should expect
this to continue in the future:

> Every generation demonstrates some events to be regular and
> predictable, which the preceding generation had declared to
> be irregular and unpredictable: so that the marked tendency of
> advancing civilization is to strengthen our belief in the uni-
> versality of order . . . it follows that if any facts, or class of
> facts, have not yet been reduced to order, we, so far from pro-
> nouncing them to be irreducible, should rather be guided by
> our experience of the past, and should admit the probability
> that what we now call inexplicable will at some future time be
> explained.[6]

In physics, Buckle argued, events that had seemed "most irreg-
ular and capricious" had been shown to follow universal laws.
"If human events were subjected to similar treatment," he insisted, "we have every right to expect similar results." The reason
no such understanding had yet been achieved, he went on to
suggest, was simply that all historians and philosophers in the past
had been "manifestly inferior" to great scientists such as Galileo,
Kepler, and Newton.

As judged by posterity, Buckle's work never quite measured up
to his own grandiose aspirations. In the two volumes of his ambitious *History of Civilization in England,* he argued that conditions

of climate and geography in different nations were influential in determining their development and wealth, and the quality of their people's intellects. More dubiously, he also concluded that Europeans were inherently superior to non-Europeans—by constitution better prepared to subdue nature, whereas others were subdued by her. Buckle certainly found no "laws" that could be verified as such by anyone in his own time or since.

In France around the same time, philosopher Auguste Comte— today considered the father of sociology—matched Buckle's enthusiasm, arguing that human events must conform to scientific laws, and that, if we could learn them, moral evils could be eliminated. Comte was convinced that mankind was finally emerging into the third of three stages of development. During a "theological" period, people explained the world in supernatural terms, and in a later "metaphysical" period, they began to put their fingers, vaguely, on some causes. Civilization, Comte believed, was finally emerging into the "positive" stage, in which man would come to see the true scientific laws that control the world. What Newton had done for the physical sciences, some other genius, or series of geniuses, would soon do for the science of man—erect a lasting scientific edifice that would displace all the philosophical claptrap that had gone before.

It goes without saying that none of this came to pass. From John Stuart Mill to Adam Smith to Karl Marx, thinkers of all persuasions have tried in vain to find "lawlike" patterns in the human world. In more recent times, dreams for a real science of man have shifted toward economic theory. I'll look more closely at economic theory and its shortcomings in a later chapter, but it suffices to point out that while our libraries groan under the weight of countless volumes of "deep" economic theory— couched in sophisticated mathematical terms—we lack any kind of understanding that would approach the level of sophistication found in an introductory textbook of physics, chemistry, or biology. Many smart people are doing economics. Considered in scientific terms, however, it is not widely capable of making accurate predictions.

A few years ago, for example, the economics consultancy London Economics assessed the recent predictions of more than thirty of the top British economic forecasting groups, including the Treasury, the National Institute, and the London Business School. They concluded:

> It is a conventional joke that there are as many different opinions about the future of the economy as there are economists. The truth is quite the opposite. Economic forecasters . . . all say more or less the same thing at the same time; the degree of agreement is astounding. The differences between forecasts are trivial relative to the differences between all forecasts and what happens . . . what they say is almost always wrong . . . the consensus forecast failed to predict any of the most important developments in the economy over the past seven years—the strength and resilience of the 1980s consumer spending boom, the depth and persistence of the 1990s recession, or the dramatic and continuing decline in inflation since 1991.[7]

Researchers have proposed thousands of ideas about the laws of crime or economic development, how cultures grow, etc., yet none has ever withstood scrutiny in the way the laws of physics have. The sciences of man are still waiting for their Kepler and Newton. But why? What makes the science of man so hard, and so much more difficult than other sciences? Maybe there is just something essentially different and unique about the human world that makes it impossible to find any "laws" for the social world? Many philosophers and social theorists have suggested as much—that, for some reason, it may all be just too complicated.

ACCIDENTS AND ARGUMENTS

To begin with, there is the irritating but unavoidable fact that tiny accidents often intrude on larger events—making disasters, wars, elections, and other important events turn out one way or another for what amounts to almost no reason at all. The British historian Edward Hallett Carr famously referred to this as the "Cleopatra's nose" problem. In Roman history, following Caesar's death, Mark Antony became infatuated with Cleopatra of Egypt and, to please her, led his ships into battle and ultimately to defeat at the hands of Octavius in the battle of Actium. Any legitimate account of the origin of that battle, and of its consequences, has to refer to Cleopatra's beauty. Winston Churchill once pointed to a version of the same irritating but fascinating "chanciness" of history: In 1920, the king of Greece died after being bitten by a pet monkey. On the ensuing chain of events that led Greece and Turkey to war, Churchill commented, "A quarter of a million persons died of this monkey's bite."

If the smallest of details continually intrude on the larger flow of human events, with the power to send it hurtling in one direction or another, how can we hope to make sense of anything? What was it, really, that led to the revival of Times Square? If Disney hadn't invested, maybe others would have stayed out as well. So it could have been the outlook of a single CEO—Disney's Michael Eisner—that was decisive. And quite possibly, his decision came down to a few words of advice from a financial adviser, or something he read in a newspaper. If there hadn't been a collapse of the Russian ruble in October of 1987, the stock market probably wouldn't have crashed. William Stern's plans would have gone forward. If they had failed to produce the desired results, Times Square today might still be down-and-out as it was in 1984. So explaining Times Square means talking about finance in Russia.

A scientific law implies some pattern that holds true from one case to the next and gives a lesson into how things work. But the existence of such laws has to seem highly suspect if tiny events can disrupt everything, pushing the future down one path or another. The problem of Cleopatra's nose suggests that the flow of human events is indeed, as someone once said, just "one damned thing after another."

There is another problem too. For an event like the revival of Times Square, we can easily imagine ten people finding ten different causes, all based on their own perspectives. A city official telling the story of the renewal will select different facts and events as being most important, as opposed to, say, the owner of a pawnshop, a policeman, or a poet who lived in the area. The trouble is, there may be thousands of contributing factors, and no one can say for sure what really matters and what doesn't. The trouble with facts, it has been said, is that there are so many of them. And it's not easy to do an experiment to find which facts really matter and which don't. So we are left with conflicting explanations, with no way to settle the debate. The dire consequences are evident on daily editorial pages of any newspaper where "conservative" and "liberal" commentators drudge up their own facts and explain the same events in entirely contradictory ways.

In the context of philosophy, and philosophers who have claimed to explain the course of human cultures, Friedrich

Nietzsche put his finger on this issue long ago, arguing that too many philosophers decide what they believe first, then go searching for reasons afterward:

> What provokes one to look at all philosophers half suspiciously, half mockingly, is not that one discovers again and again how innocent they are—how often and how easily they make mistakes and go astray; in short, their childishness and childlikeness—but that they are not honest enough in their work, although they all make a lot of virtuous noise when the problem of truthfulness is touched even remotely. They all pose as if they had discovered and reached their real opinions through the self-development of a cold, pure, divinely unconcerned dialectic (as opposed to the mystics of every rank, who are more honest and doltish—and talk of "inspiration"); while at bottom it is an assumption, a hunch, indeed a kind of "inspiration"—most often a desire of the heart that has been filtered and made abstract—that they defend with reasons they have sought after the fact. They are all advocates who resent the name, and for the most part even wily spokesmen for their prejudices, which they baptize "truths."[8]

In short, our descriptions of human events have a problem with "objectivity"—with getting everyone to agree on one description of what really happened.

There is another angle to this problem, which Carr identified as particularly problematic in the context of history. The world is infinite in detail. We are finite in our ability to select from it and to string together events. One cannot think about history without dealing in selection of some kind, but this very process brings bias into the work. As Carr suggested, the record of "facts" that

forms the basis for our stories of history reflects the selection of
the people who wrote that history:

> When I read in a modern history of the middle ages that the
> people of the middle ages were deeply concerned with reli-
> gion, I wonder how we know this, and whether it is true.
> What we know as the facts of medieval history have almost
> all been selected for us by generations of chroniclers who
> were professionally occupied in the theory and practice of
> religion, and who therefore thought it supremely important,
> and recorded everything related to it and not much else.[9]

Every journalist and anyone who reads newspapers knows
that the likes and dislikes, interests and personality, of the story-
teller influence the story he or she tells. Taking this idea to its
extreme, some contemporary "postmodern" theorists even suggest that there is no way to distinguish one "most accurate" story
about the world. Any story is as legitimate as any other. In fact,
there is no "real truth" out there to describe.[10]

But the foregoing explanations for the backwardness of the
human sciences aren't entirely convincing. Scientists in other areas such as geology and biology have to deal with similar problems, and they get along just fine. Biology has learned to deal
with the Cleopatra's nose problem—or the problem of "contingency"—which affects the living world at every turn. Chance
lies at the core of evolution, as every new generation contains
genetically novel individuals who arise through random genetic
mutation or sexual recombination. Random events ultimately lie
behind the genetic variation on which natural selection then
acts, sorting the successful from the unsuccessful. Consequently,
every organism bears in its details, visible and at the molecular

level, traces of chance events from long ago. But biologists have learned to understand the process through which chance variations, coupled with natural selection and time, lead to ordered forms such as basic body plans that show up in many organisms. Contingency doesn't prohibit accurate prediction. Biologists have also solved the problem of objectivity. All agree that the dinosaurs went extinct about sixty-five million years ago. Many factors could have played a role—changing temperatures or levels of oxygen in the atmosphere, dwindling food supplies, and so on. Researchers can't reach into the past to do experiments, but they have still been able to piece together a body of evidence that points convincingly to an asteroid impact in the Gulf of Mexico as the most likely cause of the extinction. This explanation could turn out to be wrong. But if it is, it will be replaced with a better explanation based on better evidence.

So we still haven't identified what is so uniquely difficult about understanding the human world. It's not the annoying accidents that lead to "contingency." And it's not the impossibility of doing experiments. So what is it?

THE UNGRATEFUL BIPED

There is one final argument that people often use to explain the seeming impossibility of making a human science with the power of physics—people. As individuals, we're inscrutable—intelligent yet emotional, generous yet sometimes spiteful, driven by whims and prone to delusion and error. No theory of human personality and behavior has ever been anything more than a rough sketch of the reality—something akin to the crude and fantastic maps of the world in the Middle Ages, dominated by terra incognita and whirlwinds. So it is no wonder that when you put ten of us around the dinner table, fifty within an office, or tens of millions within a nation, you get Hula Hoops and Beanie Babies, epidemics of suicide, the endless and often ridiculous machinations of politics, corruption and conspiracies, technology, hatred and war. Quite simply, we humans are the most complex things that we know about in the universe.

The situation is even worse too because we're all different, due to genetic differences and because each person has a unique history of experiences. So human science has to deal not only with individuals of near infinite complexity, but with many such individuals, all different from one another. The great Austrian physicist Wolfgang Pauli readily admitted that physics is, in this sense, far easier than social science. "In physics we can assume that every electron is identical," Pauli pointed out, "while social scientists do not have this luxury." Where would physics be if every hydrogen atom had its own unique history that left indelible traces on its behavior? What if we had to know about an atom's moods and thoughts to be able to account for its actions? It is safe to say that physics wouldn't be nearly so advanced. Physics and chemistry may be called the hard sciences, yet human science is actually far harder—in part, because of the individual complexity of people and the differences among them.

There is also, of course, the slight matter of free will. If our feeling of free will isn't an illusion, and people can really act as they please, then it seems unlikely there could be any infallible laws in the human world. Prediction would be ruled out by necessity. In the nineteenth century, Fyodor Dostoyevsky insisted that a stubborn streak in human nature would make people rebel if a science of man did ever succeed in finding laws for the human world and used them to build a perfect world. Man is the "ungrateful biped" who would, if his life were ever so constructed, immediately want to kick the whole thing over out of spite, just to prove that he could:

> Shower upon him every earthly blessing, drown him in a sea of happiness, so that nothing but bubbles of bliss can be seen on the surface; give him economic prosperity, such that he should have nothing else to do but sleep, eat cakes and busy himself with the continuation of his species, and even then out of sheer ingratitude, sheer spite, man would play you some nasty trick. He would even risk his cakes and would deliberately desire the most fatal rubbish, the most uneconomical absurdity, simply to introduce into all this positive good sense his fatal fantastic element. It is just his fantastic dreams, his vulgar folly that he will desire to retain, simply in order to prove to himself—as though that were so necessary—that men still are men and not the keys of a piano.[11]

Men will always do things that make the human world unpredictable—if even just to prove its unpredictability.

Ultimate human stubbornness is one thing. But free will interrupts prediction in a more obvious way too. Forty-five years ago, British philosopher Karl Popper argued that because free will gives us the ability to do unprecedented things—to create and invent, and to learn—this alone is enough to rule out any predictions of the future of human history. The growth of human knowledge obviously has an influence on the course of history. Look at the atomic bomb, the telephone, or the Internet. It is also true, said Popper, that we cannot predict how our knowledge will grow, for learning means discovering something new and unexpected. A future discovery that we could predict now wouldn't deserve the name. So—if changes in knowledge influence the course of history, and we cannot foresee such changes, history must be beyond prediction. "The belief in historical destiny," as Popper put it, "is sheer superstition . . . there can be no prediction of the course of human history by scientific or any other rational methods."[12]

This isn't quite the same as condemning all efforts to find patterns in the human world—Popper never went so far—but it clearly illustrates the troubles likely to be involved. Try as we might to build a "physics" of the human world, with people as the atoms, we're likely to be stymied—because the "human atom" is as complex as anything we know in the universe.

An Ultimate Barrier?

So we seem to arrive at the idea that our human world is complicated because people are complicated. In this view, we can build theories for everything else in nature—from bacterial colonies and oceanic flows to superconductors and supernovae— but there's a sharp boundary to our knowing when it comes to people. We can only make sense of human behavior and the workings of organizations, markets, cities, and governments with narrative stories and rough models of how things work, nothing that would reach the level of scientific laws or make accurate prediction possible.

This conclusion seems to entail the idea that humans somehow live "outside" nature, or at least outside scientific nature. We're not like the rest of the world. This notion actually has a long history, especially in Christian philosophy. In the Christian myth, man was created in the image of God, and as quite distinct from the rest of the natural world. We are different and special, and so one shouldn't expect science to apply to people too (at least if you're a Christian). Of course, everything in modern science points precisely in the opposite direction and has increasingly been doing so since the time of Kepler. We're not unique or different from the rest of nature; we're part of nature and follow the same principles. We share most of our DNA with field mice, and our basic genetic machinery is virtually identical to that of bacteria, who are surely our very distant evolutionary cousins. The more we learn, the more support we find for the Copernican principle: that man is an integral part of nature, but not at the center of it. We learned first that Earth is not at the center of the universe. We then learned that our solar system is no special place either, nor our galaxy, which is just one of countless millions. We learned that, biologically, we are also not special. The more we learn, the more intelligent and like us we find other animals— crows make tools, and chimpanzees have culture. We should expect to learn that humanity has a natural place in the natural world, not a special place.

As I argued in chapter 1, it is likely that much of our confusion about the human world arises not from human separation from nature, but in our mistaken belief in such separation. We've failed to be objective enough about ourselves. Adding to the trouble is our pronounced inability or unwillingness to appreciate how very simple behavior, when repeated in the interactions among many people, can be the source of exceedingly rich and surprising outcomes. By the end of this book, I hope to convince you that we can make great progress in building a science of the human world if we rectify these mistakes in our thinking; if we learn to look for patterns in the human world as we do in the rest of nature, and if we try to explain them as the natural collective outcomes of the ordinary behavior of human beings. In this sense, I think that social science today is really just embarking on the same kind of project—understanding the origins of collective patterns—with which physics has been involved for centuries.

The science best sellers often make physics out to be about string theory and the origins of the universe—which it certainly is—and yet 75 percent of all physicists work on the physics of everyday stuff, on crystals and superconductors, superfluids and magnets, plastics and rubber. This area of "condensed matter" physics explores an inexhaustible world of possibilities centered around self-organization and pattern. Put the same old atoms together in new ways and you find new substances—liquid crystals that display numbers on computer screens, plastic wires that conduct electricity. This branch of physics happens, often, to have practical consequences—new devices that create entire new industries—but this kind of physics is far more than mere technology. It is fundamentally about the exploration of the kinds of form and organization that are possible in our universe.

Of course, physicists didn't make any progress in understanding the world of condensed matter before they had a decent picture of the properties of individual atoms and molecules themselves. You have to know at least a little about the building blocks, and the same goes for social matter. So in the next few chapters we're going to start by looking at the social atom—at people as individuals and how they behave on their own and in interaction with others. In the past two decades, psychologists have probably made more progress in understanding human behavior and decision making than ever before. Modern science is gaining a much better picture of the social atom. In exploring this picture, we'll also begin to see more systematically how social atoms go together to create fashions and social classes, mass movements, and deeper social phenomena as well, including cooperation and human language. We'll see how what happened in

New York's Times Square probably had less to do with market forces than with a pattern of collective behavior that accelerates social transitions of all kinds—in human society, and in the animal kingdom as well.

There is, of course, one big difference between social and physical matter. A hydrogen atom is a hydrogen atom is a hydrogen atom, whether it is in a table, a star, or a glass of water. The atoms of physical stuff always remain the same. The social atom is very different—people change and adapt, take note of social organization and respond to it. The great philosophers who criticized the very idea of social physics were right that we do make our own choices, and that no one can predict human behavior with perfect mathematical accuracy. Yet if this makes the phenomena of social matter ultimately richer than that of physics, it is not in any way essentially different. Like physical atoms, we follow patterns just the same.

Chapter 3

OUR THINKING INSTINCTS

*The history of thought and culture is . . . a changing
pattern of great liberating ideas that inevitably turn
into suffocating straightjackets and so stimulate their
own destruction.*

—ISAIAH BERLIN[1]

O N ITS OPENING day, June 10, 2000, thousands of people
streamed over London's new Millennium Bridge—a
thousand-foot steel structure and the first pedestrian bridge
across the Thames River in central London for more than a century. Families, young professionals, small packs of teenagers, all
were enjoying the mild summer air and certainly not trying to
cause trouble. But they were unwittingly, it appears, the cause of
a near catastrophe. Around one o'clock, a policeman noticed that
the bridge, then carrying about two hundred people, seemed to
be swaying from side to side, as if in a small earthquake. There
was no earthquake. As it now seems, people's feet, in ordinary
walking, had set up a weak vibration in the bridge. That vibration then acted back on the people in a most peculiar way. To
keep their balance, people found it easier to adjust their gait and

walk in time with the gentle sway. Unfortunately, this seems to have amplified the sway. So the more the bridge swayed, the more people adjusted their gait, making the bridge sway even more, until it came to be swinging several inches to either side, all because of feedback. Fortunately, authorities managed to close the bridge before it collapsed.[2]

The social world, like the swaying Millennium Bridge, has everything to do with feedback and self-organization, with patterns that set up conditions that encourage their own further growth. In the mid to late 1980s, owners of personal computers were free to choose from a number of competing operating systems—the software that carries out a computer's housekeeping functions. You're still free to choose now, but after the rise of Microsoft, the natural forces of the marketplace push you toward using Windows. It comes already installed on many new computers, and so it's the easy choice. The more we use it, the easier it becomes to make the same choice next time. It's like walking in step with the Millennium Bridge—or buying Internet stocks in the late 1990s. Analysts worldwide were then saying that market prices were probably 20–30 percent too high, yet as investors continued buying, driving values still higher, this encouraged others to buy; they were dragged along by feedback.

Are scientists, in their work, immune from social feedback? Hardly. In the late 1970s, Australian physicist Robert May was studying simple equations used in modeling the population dynamics of predators and prey, such as foxes and rabbits. Surprisingly, he found that the outcome could fluctuate wildly and seemingly at random even with only a few simple factors at work. Before then, physicists had generally assumed that complex outcomes must reflect the action of equally complex causes. In contrast, May's example—an illustration of the phenomenon of mathematical chaos—showed otherwise and suggested that lots of complex things might be simpler than they seem.[3] Within a few years, physicists were seeing chaos everywhere—in the weather, in stock markets, in the beating of the human heart— and publishing thousands of papers on it every year. Yet the excitement was fashion as much as physics. Because chaos was a "hot" topic, it was easy to publish papers on it. The very word *chaos* gave such work an irresistible allure. Today, we see that chaos is important in many settings, but hardly the world-changing theory it once seemed. The excitement was one part science, one part social feedback.

But probably nowhere has social feedback been more powerful—and ultimately more damaging—than in the science of man. This science should obviously start with a clear understanding of how people make decisions and respond to situations in which they find themselves. More than two hundred years ago, the project got off to a promising start when the Scottish political economist Adam Smith argued that people often seek their own self-interest and do so primarily on the basis of that one faculty that sets us apart from the rest of nature—our ability to think and reason. Fifty years ago, in the postwar years, economists learned how to build an impressive mathematical framework around Smith's idea and, by taking rationality as the guide to all human action, even found a way to prove seemingly infallible mathematical theorems about some aspects of the human world. Because of its mathematical sophistication, economics has come to be seen as the model for all social science, with the assumption of perfect rationality as the prevailing fashion. Yet it's hard to look at the history of economics and not feel that economists, by focusing almost exclusively on our capacities for reasoning and calculation, got themselves bound up in a kind of intellectual straitjacket. Like those physicists who tried to reduce everything to chaos, they've tried to reduce all human behavior to rational action. They've performed intellectual and mathematical acrobatics in an effort to force everything into the confines of this one conceptual box, but it hasn't worked.

Judged by the ordinary standards of science—under which theories stand or fail on their ability to explain the real world—most economic theory, despite its sophisticated mathematics, fails in a rather embarrassing way. Fortunately, a few courageous thinkers have now stimulated a slow recovery. First and foremost, they have begun to build a far more realistic picture of the human individual—not as a rational calculating machine, as economists for so long insisted, but as a biological creature with altogether different and more flexible "thinking instincts."

THE ECONOMIC WAY OF THINKING

For most of us, the word *economics* means inflation and unemployment, or voices on the television droning on about consumer confidence. But economists see economics as the basic science of how people make decisions—to buy a Porsche rather than a Ford, to quit a job or start a family. The most important thing about us humans, economists argue, is our unique gift for reasoning. We're not slaves to our instincts, like other animals, but can use our rational capacities to weigh up the costs and benefits of any potential action. If three banks offer different rates of interest, you'll go with the one offering the most, unless another offers free checking or some other enticing advantage.

In their theories, economists tend to treat all people as close cousins of Francis Galton, the nineteenth-century English gentleman, statistician, and inventor—of a top hat with a hinged lid, for example, that could prevent overheating in a thinking man's head—who spent his life gathering facts, making measurements, and calculating. Galton ran experiments to see if prayers really work (they don't, he concluded) and compiled an exhaustive list of solutions to the problems a European traveler might encounter in "wild" countries. If you need to make a raft, what kind of wood should you use? Just consult Galton's book of 1872, *The Art of Travel*, where he has worked out the "floating powers" of alder, ash, beech, elm, fir, larch, oak, pine, poplar, and willow.[4] More than anything, Galton was a thinking man—the "rational" man, striving to meet all challenges with the power of his thinking mind. For the last fifty years, economists have argued that we're all basically the same as Galton.

In the 1960s, for example, economist Gary Becker of Columbia University began arguing that criminals might not be social misfits or moral failures, but people who have, after thoughtful analysis, simply decided that breaking the law is their best option. Lacking marketable skills, a man might well find that stealing cars or mugging old ladies is preferable to searching for a job. According to Becker's theory of "rational choice," crime is just another form of enterprise where fines and jail time have to be included among the possible costs. Becker went a lot further too. In a series of famous papers over several decades—for which he later won the Nobel Prize in economics—he argued that his theory of rational choice could explain almost everything that people do. When people change jobs, get married or divorced, or do anything else, Becker argued, it is always because they have made a rational decision to choose one action over others because it will give a better outcome. Why do people have children and invest good time and money in bringing them up? You might think of love, emotions, biology, but Becker's theory of rational choice suggests that parents are actually investing wisely in their own future, banking on getting more back from their children than they put in. "They gain from financing investments in the education and skills of children," he concluded, as long as those investments yield a higher rate of return than putting the money in the bank. "Parents can indirectly save for old age by investing in children."[5]

Theories based on this "economic way of thinking," as Becker called it, have also tended to suppose, further, that people not only try to make rational decisions, but have infinite mental capacities to do so without making errors. A typical example, and a core part of modern economics, is the so-called Life Cycle Theory of Savings. If you're forty years old and earning $60,000 a year, how much will you spend, and how much will you save? Answering questions of this kind is important for working out how much people will save in the long run, and how much they'll spend in the economy each year. In most of their models, economists assume that everyone decides how much to save in a completely rational way by estimating their year-by-year future income and then performing a complex calculation—you would need a computer to do it—to determine how much they should save this year so that their spending will be spread evenly over their entire lifetime. The model assumes not only that all people are rational, but that they are perfectly rational and make all decisions on the basis of accurate and exhaustive calculation. This is the way of standard economics. As one economist sums it up, "The cornerstone of received economic theory is the idea that human agents behave rationally. Rationality is supposed to underlie the predictability of human behavior, and thus to establish it as a candidate for systematic scientific investigation."[6] Without the assumption of unfailing human rationality, this view seems to suggest, there could not even be any human science.

This view of the human world may seem a little narrow-minded. Personally, I know that I make mistakes routinely, think silly thoughts, procrastinate, and act on emotions. If you're like most people, you do too. Ordinary people routinely act out of anger, love, or spite, with little or no calculation at all. As we'll see in this chapter, in fact, there's lots of good evidence that none of us lives up to the rational ideal of economic theory. As it turns out, most economists don't even think people really act this way either.[7] Even so, the rationality assumption still remains as the centerpiece of modern economic thinking, and there appear to be two reasons why this is the case.

Political scientist Robert Axelrod of the University of Michigan has suggested that economists have remained devoted to the rational perspective for one simple reason—without it they wouldn't know what to do. Human behavior is rich and diverse. But if we suppose everyone is perfectly rational, then everyone is also identical. Moreover, working out what people will do in any situation becomes little more than a problem in mathematics, amenable to logical deduction. "In my view," as Axelrod puts it, "the reason for the dominance of the rational choice approach is not that scholars think it is realistic . . . its unrealistic assumptions undermine much of its value as a basis for advice. The real advantage of the rational choice assumption is that it often allows deduction."[8] Rationality makes it possible to build theories with logic alone, rather than painstaking observation.

The second reason for economists' peculiar celebration of perfect rationality doesn't have to do with science and its difficulties at all, but with economists as people, and with social feedback. Economists have children, houses, careers, and if rational choice is the way everyone else is doing economics and social theory, it is natural that the quality of someone's work gets judged in those terms. In the 1970s up through the '90s, economists' models became populated by people who were increasingly rational. "The aesthetic in the field," recalls economist Richard Thaler of the University of Chicago, "became that if the agents in model A are smarter than the agents in Model B, then Model A is better than Model B."[9] If your work gets better credit if it uses perfectly rational agents, why not use them?

Some economists have even admitted the influence of this factor in their papers. One paper I read several years ago argued that it might be rational, for any individual economist, to stick with the "rational choice" idea even if he or she knows it is wrong. After all, since it is still the dominant idea, economists will do better in terms of their career by arguing for it, rather than by attacking it.

Call it what you will—a house of cards, emperor with no clothes, whatever—rational economics couldn't possibly have stood up for much longer, and it hasn't. Some economists have tried the last-ditch argument of saying that economics shouldn't be about the real world, but is *by definition* the study of perfectly rational people interacting with other perfectly rational people, making the whole thing a branch of pure mathematics. This attitude reminds me of what an aristocratic Englishwoman once said of a certain Lord Birkenhead: "He is very clever, but sometimes his brains go to his head." Other economists have, thankfully, broken ranks, preferring to work on ideas that might actually apply to the real world. Their work has proven beyond any doubt that rational choice theory is less interesting as a theory of the social world than as a social phenomenon itself. There are three important points. First, it turns out that sometimes we just cannot be rational, no matter how hard we try. Second, even when we can be rational, most of us, as a rule, aren't. And third—that's generally okay, because we have other ways to make decisions that are just as good, and often better.

A Guessing Game

One day in 1987, bankers and businessmen reading London's *Financial Times* came upon an advertisement for a weird competition. To enter, you had to choose a whole number between 0 and 100 and send it in. The winner would be the person whose number came closest to being two thirds of the average of all the numbers chosen. In case of a tie, a unique winner would randomly be chosen. The prize was a pair of round-trip tickets to fly first class on the Concorde from London to New York, valued at more than ten thousand dollars.

Imagine you were playing. How would you choose a number? According to traditional economics, you'll choose rationally. But how is that?

Obviously, you don't know what numbers other people will choose, and that makes it somewhat tricky to try to be rational. So, you might start by taking a rough guess. Maybe people's numbers will vary randomly over the entire range from 0 to 100. In that case, the average will be around 50, and so 33 would be a decent guess, as it's close to two thirds of 50. You might send this number in and hope for the best. Then again, there is clearly a problem—what if others are thinking the same way you are?

If so, then others will also choose a number around 33, and the average won't be 50, but around 33, and two thirds of that is 22. Once again, you could send this number in or follow this line of thought a little further. If others think like you, the average should be 22, so the best guess would actually be around 15, and so on. The more you think, the smaller the number should be, and the real question, obviously, is where do you stop? Continuing with this logic, you might begin to suspect that everyone will choose a very small number, maybe even 0. And in fact, that would be a curiously fitting outcome, as everyone's choice would really then be two thirds of the average, since 0 is two thirds of 0. As it turns out, 0 is what a rational economist would choose. But would anyone else?

As it turns out, yes, but not many. This curious competition was set up by Richard Thaler of the University of Chicago, and when he tabulated the entries he found that a handful of people had really chosen 0, while quite a few chose 33 and 22—stopping the logic after one or two steps. The overall average was 18.9 and the winner had chosen 13.

The point of Thaler's competition was to illustrate a glaring inconsistency between how rational economics says people behave and how they really behave. The idea that people should choose 0 comes from a part of economic tradition known as game theory, which looks at how rational people can best act in competitive situations. In the 1950s, mathematician John Nash—protagonist of the recent film *A Beautiful Mind*—proved that for many situations there is always a "best" strategy that a rational person can use, knowing that his opponents are all rational too. For Thaler's competition, that strategy is to choose 0. After all, if everyone is perfectly rational, they will all choose the same number, and 0 is the only number that would be equal to two thirds of the average.

The trouble is, a rational economist taking part in the competition is a certain loser—which is actually neither rational nor very smart. What it would be is naïve, especially about the nature of human behavior. An economist can try to be rational himself, but he cannot control what others do. The competition isn't a problem in pure mathematics, for the best number depends on the actual numbers that people choose, for whatever crazy reasons they might have. As a result, game theory of the rational variety couldn't be more irrelevant. And what makes that important is that we face situations similar to Thaler's competition every day, in which reason and logic simply cannot cope with the real world.

Driving to work in the morning, you may want to choose a road that others won't take, so as to avoid traffic. But so do other people. As a result, you have lots of people trying to do what most other people won't do—an impossible task, rationally, if people can't read minds. Or think of buying and selling stocks, where big money is at stake and you might think rational action should always pay off. It doesn't. An old argument in economics holds that stock prices must always have their fair, realistic values because investors, being rational, will buy up any momentarily undervalued stocks, making their prices rise, or will sell any overvalued stocks, until their prices fall. Rational investors will do so because they can make easy money in the process. But it's not so simple. Suppose some clever people notice that a particular stock is priced way too low. To make easy money, they might rationally try to buy the stock, with the idea of holding it until the price comes up to its right value, and then to sell at a profit. But like a rational economist in Thaler's game, they might be right about the stock, but naïve about people. Completely uninformed, irrational investors, thinking for no good reason the stock is a loser, might continue selling it and drive its price down even more, no matter how ridiculous and irritating that may be.

A perfectly rational investor can lose money because the stock market runs on beliefs about other people's beliefs and so is a

weird setting to try to be rational. If enough people start thinking that the temperature in Cleveland influences the market, it
will begin to influence the market, and a wise investor had better
check the weather before buying and selling, no matter how "irrational" that may be. So much for rationality—it's a tool that
can only be used some of the time, even in principle.[10]

But for anyone who might hope to save the theory of rational
choice, a little further investigation only makes things much, much
worse. As it turns out, even in situations where a child could do the
calculation required to make a logical decision, many of us don't.
We seem genetically hardwired for error.

INSTINCTS FOR ERROR

Suppose I tell you that a bat and ball, together, cost a total of
$1.10, and that the bat costs $1 more than the ball. How much is
the ball? This problem obviously doesn't require sophisticated
calculating skills. It's no more difficult than problems school-
children solve every day in their lessons. But a few years ago,
when MIT psychologist Shane Frederick posed this question to
bright students at Princeton University and the University of
Michigan, and gave them plenty of time to work out the answer,
50 percent of those at Princeton and 56 percent at Michigan gave
wrong answers. They said the bat costs $1 and the ball $0.10, or
10 cents, rather than giving the right answer—that the bat costs
$1.05 and the ball $0.05, or 5 cents.

Almost everyone, when first asked this question, wants to
blurt out the 10-cent answer. Somehow, it just feels right. Visu-
ally, the total of $1.10 splits easily into $1 and $0.10, and these
two quantities differ by roughly the right amount. So the 10-cent
answer, for our minds, is something like a "natural" solution—it

takes a conscious effort not to give in and a stronger effort to find the right answer. Pose the problem differently, and it's not so hard. If I tell you the bat and ball cost $1.10 together, and the bat costs $1.05, your instincts won't miss.

There is obviously no "rational choice" explanation for this experiment, or for hundreds of others like it that psychologists and experimentally minded economists have run over the past decade. If you want to explain them, you have to look elsewhere, and a good place to start is what Princeton psychologist Daniel Kahneman refers to as the "two systems" of our mental apparatus.[11] Kahneman argues that only part of our mind is rational. This part can process information consciously and on the basis of logic. It works slowly, step-by-step, and only with constant effort and attention. But this calculating mind rides atop another more "instinctual" mind that is fast, automatic, and difficult to control. Our instinctual mind sees $1.10 and splits it into $1 and $0.10. It grabs hold of key details and spits out an answer with a "shoot first ask questions later" style that doesn't require any "rational" analysis.

Kahneman as much as anyone else is responsible for beginning the gradual unraveling of the rational delusions of economics. In the 1970s and 1980s, working with the late Amos Tversky, Kahneman explored lots of simple situations in which our instincts for thinking affect how we take in information and use it, and how intelligent people depart systematically from economists' rational ideal. For example, they found that how a question or situation is "framed" or presented can have dramatic effects on how people deal with it. Patients who are told that a dangerous operation has a 90 percent chance of success are more likely to go for it than if they are told it has a 10 percent rate of failure. Framing can similarly influence how much you value a bit of money. Suppose you're buying a CD for $15 and the clerk says you can get it for $5 less at their other store two minutes away. Many people will make the effort to save the $5. But studies find that many of those same people won't bother if the product they're purchasing is a leather jacket for $125. Five dollars is $5, rationally, but the instinctual mind doesn't agree—it judges that $5 is worth more in one case than in the other.

This is, of course, completely irrational. But it is quintessentially human. And things get a lot worse if you move from really simple questions to those cloaked in the dry and dusty language of statistics. Today's blood tests for HIV are incredibly accurate. If someone is HIV-positive, the test says so with 99.9 percent accuracy. If someone doesn't have HIV, the test is even better—it says so with 99.99 percent accuracy. Now, take a random person off the U.S. streets—someone who isn't an intravenous drug user, male homosexual, or otherwise known to be a high-risk candidate for having HIV—and test them for HIV. If they test positive, what's the chance they really do have the virus? This seems like a no-brainer. It's almost certain that person has HIV. Right? Wrong. The right answer is one half, or only a 50 percent chance.

If you gave the wrong answer, don't feel too bad. Psychologist Gerd Gigerenzer of the Max Planck Institute in Germany has presented this problem to hundreds of people, from students to mathematicians and experienced doctors. Even the experts get it wrong. He found, for example, that about 95 percent of the college-level students gave the wrong answer. As many as 40 percent of the doctors got it wrong, even though they've had specific training in dealing with just these kinds of issues.[12] The problem is with our thinking instincts.

If you're like most people, in fact, your instinctual mind has already taken control and can't see that I haven't yet given you enough information even to formulate a rational answer. To do so, you need to remember that the "random person," at the outset, is unlikely to be HIV positive, as the virus infects only 0.01 percent of the U.S. population not belonging to a high-risk group—male homosexuals, intravenous drug users, and so on. This means that the chance this person will have the virus and (almost certainly) test positive is also just 0.01 percent. That turns out to be equal to the chance this person doesn't have the virus but will test positive by a rare mistake. So a positive outcome is just as likely to be true as false. If this still seems obscure, it's probably because probabilities tend to confuse the human mind. Think in terms of numbers of people instead. Imagine that about ten thousand people not obviously at high risk for having HIV come into a clinic for tests. Given the prevalence of the virus in the ordinary, non-high-risk population (roughly one in ten thousand), it is likely that one person will actually have the virus; they will almost certainly test positive, because the test is so accurate. The other 9,999 people won't have the virus. But because the test isn't absolutely perfect—it gives a false positive one in ten thousand tries—it is likely that one of these people will also test positive. The test has far more chances to give false positives than to give false negatives. Over all, out of ten thousand, we should find roughly one true positive and one false positive—a positive result is true only 50 percent of the time.

All in all, it's not our rationality that stands out, but our routine departures from it. Many economists like to talk about these departures as "anomalies," as if they are weird and inexplicable deviations from the rational ideal. But a deeper perspective suggests that our thinking instincts may not actually be anomalous at all. In the context of human history, our errant ways may make perfect sense.

Modern Skulls, Stone Age Minds

The trouble with rational choice is that it sees the human mind as an all-purpose computer—as an ultrapowerful device that you, the owner, can set on any task you like. But the mind isn't an all-purpose computer. It does some things better and more easily than others. It recognizes in a flash the back of a friend's head at fifty yards, but struggles to calculate 223 times 57. Think of the human heart. It's an exquisite pump for pushing blood around through our arteries and veins, but it is not an all-purpose pump. It would do a terrible job of pumping the oil through your car's engine. The heart was designed by evolution for a specific task, so too the human mind.

A better metaphor for the mind would be a bizarre machine that now stands in the museum of science in London. Its heavy wooden structure, standing around six feet high, supports a series of steel wheels of various sizes. These link through metal shafts to a central point below, where a mechanical pen can trace marks on a rotating drum. If you turn a crank on the machine, the wheels all spin, as does the drum, and the pen draws out a wavering, curvy line—the curve goes up and down, not quite regularly, but almost. If you read the plaque below the machine, you'll see that this device was invented by British physicist William Thomson in the late nineteenth century and was used, until around 1950, to predict the schedule of the tides. The wheels of different sizes contributed variations to reflect the influence of the moon, the sun, and other factors, and the mechanism put them all together to calculate the total tide.

This machine couldn't be used to do much else. It is not a computer, as it cannot be programmed. This is what makes it a better metaphor for the human mind, which, like this machine, is a specialized device designed for specific tasks.

The brain is the physical product of millions of years of evolution and bears, in its structure and function, the traces of all that history. It didn't evolve to solve mathematical problems, steer automobiles, or judge the sense of risky financial investments. It certainly didn't evolve to see through forests of complex statistical reasoning. Our brains evolved to solve the kinds of problems that our ancestors faced in a very different world, and when it comes to understanding the social atom, the single most important fact is that our ancestors, for 99 percent of human history, lived in small, nomadic bands of hunter-gatherers—typically a few dozen people. They were, as anthropologist John Tooby puts it, "on a camping trip that lasted an entire lifetime" and survived by gathering plants or hunting animals.[13] Evolution by natural selection would gradually have favored changes in the human brain that helped our ancestors solve the most pressing day-to-day problems—hunting, finding mates, raising children, recognizing whom they could trust and who might be dangerous.

You wouldn't expect Thomson's machine to be good at doing calculations for aircraft navigation. It was designed for something else. The human mind has a similar problem in dealing with the modern world, as we're more adapted to the conditions of our hunter-gatherer ancestors than to our current conditions. We haven't yet had time to adapt, and this leads to some bizarre situations. Our ancestors learned to fear snakes, as these were important dangers in the dense tropical forests of Africa. Today, spiders and snakes still terrify many people, yet hardly anyone has powerful fears of electrical sockets or riding in automobiles, which generally pose a far more serious risk. Our minds are special-purpose information-processing machines designed to provide us with thinking instincts tuned to our ancestors' world. As Tooby puts it, "They make certain kinds of inferences just as easy, effortless, and 'natural' to us as humans, as spinning a web is to a spider."

Another peculiar human behavioral habit is "loss aversion." Rationality demands that people should like winning $10 as much as they hate losing $10—there should be symmetry in valuing equal-sized gains and losses. But this isn't the case. Take the decisions of participants on the television game *Who Wants to be a Millionaire*, for example. Here people face a sequence of multiple-choice questions and keep going until they answer wrong. A player's potential winnings double at each stage, but they also face greater potential losses. A couple of years ago, economist Gauthier Lanot of Queen's University in Belfast and colleagues analyzed the behavior of 515 participants in the UK version of the game. Only three went all the way to win £1 million, roughly two thirds quit while they were winning, while only one third ended the game by gambling on a question and getting it wrong. The researchers' analysis showed that more people would have won a million—and contestants would have taken home more overall—had they gambled more. A rational player, on average, would win more than do real people, who are especially averse to large losses. Curiously, other researchers have seen similar loss aversion in primates in the laboratory. At Yale University, psychologist Laurie Santos and economist Keith Chen offered capuchin monkeys various gambles involving grapes. By manipulating the details of the experiment, they could make the very same gamble seem like a potential win for the monkey (get one grape for sure, with half a chance for another) or as a potential loss (get two grapes for sure, with half a chance for losing one of them). Despite the strict equivalence of the two situations, the monkeys strongly preferred the former setup, with payoffs framed as a potential win, rather than a potential loss.[14] The similarity between human and primate irrationality suggests a deep evolutionary origin.

So when it comes to human behavior and decision making, we shouldn't be surprised that rationality isn't the final answer. The action of our instinctual brain often takes place out of view of our conscious minds, which may indeed have only the illusion of control. Perhaps the most famous, and controversial, experiment to suggest this somewhat unnerving idea was performed by German psychologist Benjamin Libet in the 1980s.[15] Libet and colleagues used electrodes to monitor brain activity in the cerebral cortex of volunteers as they made decisions and took simple actions, such as pressing a button. During a fixed interval, the volunteers could press the button whenever they liked and were to note the precise moment when they first felt the emotional impulse to do so. The researchers found that the volunteers typically pressed the button about one fifth of a second after first being aware of their decision and intention to do so. The real surprise was that the recordings showed brain activity shooting up a half second earlier, a good three hundred milliseconds before the subject was ever conscious of any impulse to push the button. This seems to suggest a complete reversal of how we think our minds work. We think the conscious mind makes a decision, sends out commands, and the body responds, moving arms and fingers in response. Libet's experiment instead suggested that the awareness of the conscious decision came only after the volunteers had already begun the mental operations required to push the button. In this experiment, at least, the conscious mind wasn't in control, it only had that illusion.

The upshot is that we should really take Kahneman's idea of "two systems" quite seriously. When we first face some new situation, our instantaneous response flows out of our instinctual system. For that moment, we're hunter-gatherers in the modern world, the close evolutionary cousins of capuchin monkeys, getting by with the mental tools our ancestors handed down to us. Only later, slowly, haltingly, and with uncertain success, does our second mental apparatus, our inner Francis Galton, bring reason to the table. Think again of those students at Princeton and the University of Michigan trying to decide on the prices of the bat and the ball. Their thinking instincts, honed by evolution to spot patterns quickly and efficiently, saw in a snap how to break $1.10 into quantities of the right size. Half gave an answer based only on their instincts. Another half, with the second system, managed to override their instincts, and they got the right answer.

Perfect rationality exists outside of space and time. People do not. And therein lies the problem with seeing people as rational automatons or calculating machines. We're part of a human race with a long evolutionary history, hunter-gatherers dressed in modern clothes, instinctual thinkers with weak calculating machines tacked on.

EVOLUTIONARY MAN

Until recently, economics (and here I speak of it in its traditional and "hyperrational" incarnation) was widely considered to be the right framework for understanding the social world. Researchers in psychology, evolutionary biology, and economics itself have now realized that they were living a collective dream. Ten years ago, political scientist Francis Fukayama could write that prevailing economic theory based on the idea of rational choice was "about 80 percent right."[16] Today, it looks a lot closer to being 80 percent wrong, even just considering problems that stem from its

focus on rational behavior (we'll see some further serious problems in later chapters). But this book, ultimately, isn't about tear-
ing down, it is about building up a better theory of the social
world. And that starts with a better picture of the social atom.

To make a rough summary, we could say that Kahneman's
"two systems" correspond to two essential principles that account for an awful lot of human behavior, at least when it comes
to solving problems.

First, we're not rational calculators, but crafty gamblers. Gut feelings,
emotions, suspicions—where do they come from? From the
hunter-gatherers locked inside who see and sense in ways our
conscious minds do not. We are alive today because our ancestors
had hardwired into their behavior a set of simple rules for making decisions that gave pretty good results—enough for their
survival—but have little to do with rational calculation. We do
the same. The rational spirit of Francis Galton seems to reside in
only one small portion of our psyche; the rest seems to be ruled
by ancient spirits making quick and brutal judgments with little
time for nuance and subtlety.

Second, we are adaptive opportunists. If rational thinking isn't nearly
as important as economists used to think, it isn't completely unimportant either. Part of our mind does work with reason and logic,
and it can help keep our instinctual system from getting us into
trouble. Even so, what really makes the conscious part of our mind
powerful isn't logic but the ability to adapt—to take a step based on
one rule, idea, or belief, then to adjust depending on the outcome.
Rational thinking itself usually means following mental trails of
trial and error so as to proceed from some first guess toward a series
of progressively better answers. This is the real secret of our intelligence: our ability to follow simple steps and to adjust and learn. If
you don't know the solution, don't worry. Try something, because

by interacting with the world, you learn from it. Even rationality is an empirical process.

In coming chapters, I'll find it useful to refer to these rough rules, making them a little more specific here and there as the occasion demands. They paint a picture of human behavior that, satisfyingly, doesn't stand apart from the rest of the living world. And they provide a basis to begin understanding our social physics. To begin boldly, we might begin with the financial markets—the one setting where one might naturally expect traditional economics to be on its firmest ground.

Chapter 4

THE ADAPTIVE ATOM

*How do humans reason in situations that are com-
plicated or ill-defined? Modern psychology tells that
as humans we are only moderately good at deductive
logic, and we make only moderate use of it. But
we are superb at seeing or recognizing or matching
patterns—behaviours that confer obvious evolutionary
benefits. In problems of complication, then, we look for
patterns.*

—Brian Arthur[1]

IN DECEMBER 1992, former Salomon Brothers vice chair-
man John Meriwether set out to put together a financial all-
star team to make a killing in the markets. In his thirty-year
career, Meriwether had garnered a reputation as an unusually
savvy bond trader and exceptional financial engineer. He proved
equally adept as a recruiter. Meriwether started boldly, hiring
economists Myron Scholes and Robert Merton, winners of the
Nobel Prize for a brilliant mathematical theory that allows analysts to calculate the correct price for complex "derivatives." A
derivative is a contract—for example, one that gives its owner the

option to buy a certain stock next year at today's current price. You can buy and sell such contracts just as easily as you can simple stocks. But how much is an option worth? This is clearly a little trickier.

A stock's value should, ideally, reflect the legitimate prospects a company has for making profits and paying dividends. The value of an option contract, however, depends on the value of the stock in question, and also on the prospects for that value to go up or down between now and next year when the option comes due. But Merton and Scholes (working with another economist, the late Fischer Black) showed how mathematics can reduce some of that uncertainty and give traders exact knowledge of an option's most likely worth in terms of the value of its underlying stock.[2] Their elegant theory, it has been said, did "for trading and investment what the Apollo space program did for lunar exploration" and led directly to an explosion in derivatives trading during the 1980s. So Meriwether knew what he was doing when he put these big brains together with a handful of other Wall Street wizards to manage a new hedge fund, Long-Term Capital Management. Their aim was to make virtually risk-free profits by pouncing on temporary "inefficiencies" in world markets.

Meriwether had little trouble assembling initial investors, and in the first two years, 1994 and 1995, the fund returned net profits of more than 40 percent. Things only went better in coming years, and by November 1997, LTCM was able to reward its investors with a windfall of nearly $2.7 billion in "excess capital." By early 1998, LTCM had increased its portfolio of assets to $130 billion. To market analysts, it seemed as if LTCM had discovered the secret for pumping money out of markets without any chance of loss. But then something went dreadfully wrong. In

September of 1998, "unexpected" volatility in the markets, set off in part by Russia's default on its debt, led LTCM to lose more than 90 percent of its value. As the fund had borrowed more than $125 billion, these losses sent ripples through the global economy. To avoid a more widespread collapse in the financial markets, the Federal Reserve Bank of New York organized a $3.6 billion bailout.[3]

What went wrong? Philosophers, historians, and others who think carefully about the nature of explanation, and about the links between cause and effect, like to distinguish between "proximate" causes and "ultimate" causes. If someone drives off a bridge one night, the proximate cause of death may be the dismembering impact at the bottom of the ravine. But if the driver was known to have habitually driven while drunk, the ultimate cause might be found in that habit, which made a fatal crash almost certain, only leaving fate to fill in the particular details. In the case of LTCM, the proximate cause of its demise was the unusual financial trouble in Russia, which no one had foreseen. Those within LTCM likened it to a once-in-a-hundred-year freak storm that wrecked their otherwise faultlessly designed and managed craft.

But what about the ultimate cause? Ironically, for all its mathematical sophistication, it seems that LTCM had failed to take proper account of a curious discovery of mathematicians some thirty years before—that financial markets of all kinds, from the NYSE to the German DAX, have an inherent predisposition toward unexpectedly large fluctuations. If it hadn't been the crisis in Russia, it seems, LTCM would have been sunk sooner or later by something else. In markets, it turns out, freak storms just aren't as freaky as we think they should be. Understanding why means coming to grips with the collective implications of one of our most obvious traits—our ability to learn and adapt.

FAT TAILS

Suppose the price of oil today is $64 a barrel. What will it be, say, one month from now? You might speculate about international politics or the tenuous state of crucial pipelines in Ukraine, but there is no way to know for sure—this is a matter for statistics. The traditional way of answering was laid down more than a century ago, oddly enough by a French physicist, Louis Bachelier, in an unusual Ph.D. thesis entitled "Theory of Speculation." Bachelier supposed that if you recorded the changes in the price of any stock over many intervals—a day, a month, whatever—you would find that these numbers should fall onto the "bell curve," well-known from high school mathematics (see figure 4). There will be an average price change, reflected by the central peak of the curve, where the numbers fall most frequently. The curve then drops off quickly to either side, indicating that extremely large price changes, either up or down, are rare. Everything from IQ scores to dice games works to the tune of the bell curve, and

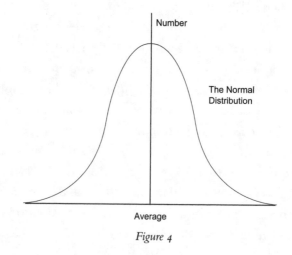

Number

The Normal
Distribution

Average

Figure 4

mathematicians even refer to it as the "normal" distribution, since it seems to be the way things "usually" work in nature.[4]

Bachelier's idea is obvious—changes in financial prices work just like everything else. Modern economists have generally followed his perspective, while unpacking its logic a bit further. As we saw in the last chapter, if people are more or less rational, stock prices shouldn't generally be too out of whack with their realistic values. If a stock's price changes, the argument goes, it must be because "new information" has hit the market—a corporation has changed key management, perhaps, or discovered a new oil field. You cannot predict these things in advance. And when there are lots of new things going on, and all kinds of new information, coming from different sources and for entirely different reasons, the net outcome should be stock changes that follow the bell curve.[5]

From all this comes one conclusion—that prices should follow a gentle "random walk," bouncing up and down by small amounts. If some set of events or objects conforms to the bell curve, you should hardly ever come across a value wildly different from the average. When it comes to people, you should see lots of people weighing 150 pounds, an occasional 300-pounder, but never one who tips the scales at 2,000 pounds. For changes in the price of oil, wheat, automobiles, or anything else, the bell curve picture suggests, similarly, that prices should also go up or down by small amounts, 0.5 percent, 1 percent, and so on, with large changes of, say, 10–20 percent in a single day being unlikely.

Because prices in Bachelier's picture jump around randomly, much like real stock prices, his theory seemed plausible; so plausible, in fact, that no one ever checked it against data from real financial markets until 1963. That's when another Frenchman, mathematician Benoit Mandelbrot, working at IBM research, found a rather shocking surprise.

Mandelbrot was looking at price fluctuations for cotton as listed on the Chicago Mercantile Exchange. Measuring price differences over days or weeks, he tallied up how often he saw changes of different sizes, then plotted the numbers. The pattern he found looks like the bell curve, except for one important difference—the "tails" drop off to zero much more slowly (see figure 5). Technically, mathematicians refer to the pattern Mandelbrot found as a "power law." What is important for the moment is that this curve falls off so slowly that extreme events aren't nearly as rare as one would expect on the basis of "normal" statistics.[6] Forty years later, we know the same goes for oil, pork bellies, or stocks. You find the same pattern also in the stocks of individual companies listed on the New York Stock Exchange, or in the famous Standard & Poor's 500 stock index.[7] You find it in other stock markets,[8] in Japan and Germany, in foreign-exchange markets,[9] and in bond markets. The evidence is overwhelming—in markets of all kinds, extreme changes happen far more frequently than they "should" according to normal statistics.

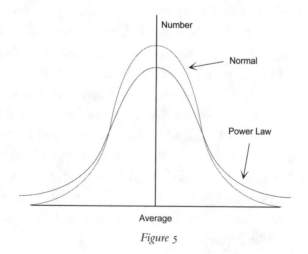

Figure 5

No theory of economics or finance has ever been able to explain this in a convincing way. One popular idea is that most extreme movements might simply be due to "external shocks," destabilizing events such as the terrorist attacks of 9/11, or major corporate or government scandals. Events can obviously rock the markets and must be the cause of some large movements, but the general explanation doesn't seem to wash, because many large movements seem to take place in the absence of any big event. In 1991, when a group of economists examined the fifty largest one-day price movements in the United States in the years since World War II, they found that many of them happened on days when there was no big news.[10]

So the fat-tail puzzle remains, which is rather embarrassing for economics—after all, what can economics hope to explain if not markets? The puzzle is more than academic too. Merton, Scholes, and the other financial wizards at LTCM had tried to estimate how likely it was that they might get whacked by a large fluctuation in the market, but did so using "ordinary" statistics, a product of economists' rational faith. For market fluctuations, the bell curve predicts that one-day drops of 10 percent in the value of a stock should only happen about once every five hundred years. Real-world data gives a more reliable estimate: about once every five years, which turned out to be a little too often for LTCM to get away with its trading strategy.

How do we understand fat tails? As I argued last chapter, one of the primary behavioral characteristics of the social atom is acting on the basis of simple rules, while benefiting from on-the-fly adaptability. This is hardly news. But it is by no means obvious to what such adaptability might lead when you put many people together. As it turns out, bringing this perspective into the theory of markets is quite enough, on its own, to account for Mandelbrot's mystery.

DRINKING AT THE EL FAROL BAR

In the summer of 1992, Irish musician Gerry Carty played every Thursday evening at the El Farol bar in Santa Fe, New Mexico. Stanford University economist Brian Arthur had recently taken a position at the new Santa Fe Institute, an interdisciplinary center for science, located just down the road. Arthur liked the bar and the music and often spent enjoyable evenings there. While there, he also ran across a curious social puzzle.

Arthur had a great time at the El Farol on some evenings, when a good crowd showed up, but there were still at least some seats left. On other evenings, however, the place was over-crowded, and the stifling heat and noise made him, along with everyone else, miserable. Unfortunately, attendance seemed to fluctuate wildly from week to week, with no obvious pattern, so the decision to go, or not to go, became a sort of weekly dilemma for Arthur: he wanted to go, but only on evenings when he thought most others would not go. As he realized, anyone else who liked the bar faced the same dilemma—everyone trying to do what most others don't do, in a situation a lot like Richard Thaler's competition of guessing numbers. Both problems melt the gears off the engine of rationality.

But people do make decisions in such situations. They reach into the bag of coping tricks that evolutionary biology has pro-vided and find some way to make a decision, rational or not. Arthur soon found himself thinking about the process of think-ing. What does that bag of thinking tricks contain? What do people pull out of it, and why? And how might this explain what happened at the bar?

Think of El Farol attendance as a natural phenomenon, and suppose you have to come up with some theory to explain it. How would you proceed? First, you'll need some way to model how people make their decisions. What kinds of information will they look at in trying to pick nights that won't be totally overcrowded? You'll also need to consider that not everyone thinks alike; different people make decisions on different principles. Ponder this for a while, and you might have some sympathy for those economic theorists who made a religion of rationality. At least it makes theorizing about people *possible*. If people aren't rational, they might do just about anything, leading to a concert of human chaos, with any hope of a theory, it seems, going out the window. But Arthur, in an inspired moment, saw a way past this imposing barrier.

By chance, Arthur had been reading an old paper from the 1960s by psychologist Julian Feldman. Feldman had argued that the way people make most decisions has little to do with logic, and a lot to do with using simple rules and learning by trial and error. In particular, people try to recognize patterns in the world and use them to predict what might come next. At the end of the 2005–6 National Football League season, for example, the Washington Redskins reeled off five straight victories to make the play-offs. Look into the newspapers and you'll see that to some commentators, this pattern meant that the team was "peaking at just the right time" and would probably do well in the play-offs. To others, in contrast, the streak of wins had caused such an emotional strain that the now tired Redskins would easily be beaten. These two theories take an observed pattern and use it to make predictions about the future.

Following Feldman, and translating this into the setting of El Farol, Arthur reckoned that some people might think the bar will be overcrowded this week if it was overcrowded last week. Others might believe just the opposite—that if many people went last week, they'll probably stay away this week, leaving a more reasonable number of people in the bar. You can imagine a near infinity of such "theories" that people might believe about how recent bar attendance, over several weeks perhaps, gives signals about the future. But there is also a second element to this "theory"- or "hypothesis"-driven style of behavior. People aren't inflexible idiots, and they will quickly abandon some idea if it sends them to an utterly jammed El Farol four weeks running. Feldman had argued that people tend to hold a number of hypotheses in their heads at once, and to act on whichever seems to be making the most sense at the time. This has an obvious resonance with our everyday experience. One of the best ways to go about a task, anything from putting up some shelves to finding a job, is often to just get started, even if you have no clear idea of the best way to proceed. You try something, then you learn and adapt. "The world," as Jacob Bronowski once put it, "can only be grasped by action, not by contemplation." Following this way of thinking, Arthur replaced rationality with a view of people as acting on the basis of simple theories, while adapting along the way.

To see what such rule-based, adaptive behavior might lead to, he then turned to the computer. Arthur first made up a long list of possible theories, such as the following:

1. Attendance will be the same as last week.
2. The bar will be overcrowded this week if it wasn't overcrowded last week (and vice versa).

3. The bar will be crowded this week only if it was not crowded three weeks in a row.

4. Attendance will be the same as it was four weeks ago.

Obviously, many such theories are possible. To make a model of El Farol, Arthur supposed (arbitrarily) that one hundred people might go to the bar, and he gave each person ten hypotheses selected at random. He then programmed the computer to have each person keep track of how well each of their ten hypotheses did in recent weeks—how well they predicted bar attendance, that is—and to use the best one to decide whether to go to the bar. In other words, the computer agents, like real people, could keep several ideas in mind and use whichever seemed to be working best. "Best," in this case, meant getting them to the bar on nights when it wasn't overcrowded—Arthur set this limit at sixty people—and keeping them home on nights when it was.

Arthur's model for El Farol represents a crude way to put into action one of the ideas of the last chapter—that we're adaptive rule followers, rather than rational automatons. But the model is surprisingly realistic.[11] In simulations, Arthur found that the number of people going to the bar quickly settled around an average of sixty—the number he had defined as the limit before the bar was crowded. But bar attendance didn't settle exactly at sixty; rather, it continued to bounce up and down from week to week (see figure 6), and it is not hard to see why.[12] People do well in this game by being in the minority—going to the bar when most others stay home and vice versa. Now suppose there is some pattern in the attendance, and a few players, acting on it, consistently put themselves into the minority. This can only work for so long, because other players will gradually adapt, noticing this pattern themselves, and also join the minority. The minority will grow

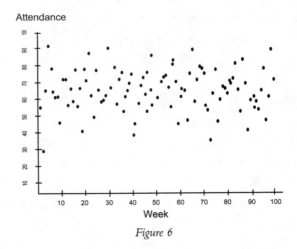

Figure 6

as others learn the pattern and join until the minority becomes the majority—and all these people begin to suffer. Any pattern that arises in the group will naturally stir up behaviors among the agents that will ultimately wipe it out—a perverse situation indeed.

Could this possibly have something to do with financial markets, especially with their incessant fluctuations that seem to defy predictions? Or possibly with their proclivity toward large events that lack an obvious "external" cause?

AN UNREASONABLE EFFECTIVENESS

In an essay written in 1960, the great physicist Eugene Wigner speculated about what he called the "unreasonable effectiveness of mathematics in the natural sciences." Wigner told a fictional story about two high school friends who, years later, were talking about their jobs. One had become a statistician of human population trends and showed some of his recent work, packed with equations, to his friend, who soon became skeptical. "What is this symbol here?" he asked, pointing to the symbol for pi, which appeared in one of the formulas. The statistician explained that pi represents the ratio of the circumference of the circle to its diameter. "Now you've gone too far," his friend exclaimed, laughing. "Details of the human population surely have nothing to do with the circumference of the circle!"[13]

Indeed, how can the geometry of the circle possibly have anything to do with the statistics of people? No one, as far as I know, has ever really explained it. Equally bizarre, perhaps, is the way mathematical models inspired by one problem so often turn out to be useful in others that seem totally different. Arthur's bar game offers a stunning illustration.

Many people who invest in stocks are known as chartists— they look to the charts of past price movements and try to spot patterns that can help them predict future movements. They behave a lot like Arthur's bar-goers, only they look to a pattern of prices rather than attendance. Prices can go up or down, just as the bar can be crowded or empty, and investors can buy or sell stocks, just as people can choose to go to the bar or stay home. Because of this similarity, the model of El Farol can be transformed into a toy model of a market with only one key addition—a price.

A fundamental truth of any market is that prices go up or down because of an imbalance between supply and demand. If more people want to buy a stock than sell it, its price should go up, and vice versa. In the latter half of the 1990s, Arthur and several colleagues, including economist Blake LeBaron and physicist Richard Palmer, used this idea to turn El Farol into an extremely simple, yet adaptive model of a financial market. In their virtual market, as in El Farol, were agents who kept track of a handful of theories at each moment and used whichever seemed to be working best to decide whether to buy or sell stock. Every such theory predicted, by looking at the record of past prices, what would happen to prices in the future. To complete the model, Arthur and colleagues supposed that the price at any moment would go up if there are more people wanting to buy than sell, and vice versa. The full logic was simple: past patterns of prices influence investors' current decisions, and those current decisions—by setting up an imbalance in buyers and sellers— drive new movements in prices, creating an ongoing spiral of cause and effect.

To test the realism of their idea, Arthur and the others set up another computer model and let it run. The outcome, given the simplicity of the model, is quite surprising. The price in their ar- tificial market bounced up and down irregularly, sometimes quite violently and abruptly, all by virtue of the internal dynamics of the interacting, adaptive agents. Their model generates a market with winners and losers, exciting rallies and crashes, and an emo- tional mood of its own. In qualitative terms, the market looks realistic—and conspicuously, without any external shocks what- soever.[14] This qualitative match alone is quite a victory, as the model stands on a plausible, if vastly oversimplified, picture of individual human behavior. But there is more. Arthur and his colleagues ran statistical analyses à la Mandelbrot to check the mathematical character of their market's fluctuations. Running it hundreds of times, varying the kinds of hypotheses the agents used, how far back in time they looked when trying to make pre- dictions, and a number of other details in the model, the re- searchers found that none of this mattered much. Without any special "tuning," but quite naturally, the model always gave rise to the fat-tailed propensity for large fluctuations seen in real markets.

So it seems that what rationality cannot explain, a mystery of half a century, finds a natural explanation in adaptive behavior and self-organization. Arthur didn't have to solve any deep technical mysteries or invent new mathematics. His model, in fact, is extremely crude, yet it works because it gets one important thing right—it replaces implausible perfect rationality with plausible adaptive learning. The fat tails then emerge as naturally as those stone rings in the arctic tundra. The major ups and downs in this market cannot be traced to any external shocks or to the actions of any one person. They don't have any easily identifiable cause in some "perverse" aspect of human behavior. Rather, the tendency for large fluctuations, a universal feature of all markets, emerges out of the way the agents, the atoms of this world, organize themselves into a delicate pattern of interdependence. Understanding why one rally is really big while another is small means getting down into the complex ecology of theories or hypotheses in the minds of all the traders, seeing how the actions of one trader, by influencing the prices, changed the behavior of others, or did not.

Since Arthur and his colleagues' early demonstration, many further studies have elaborated upon it and look to be bringing market theory into an exciting era marked by much greater realism and accuracy.[15] And this success illustrates an important point about good scientific thinking. Fifty-three years ago, economist Milton Friedman argued that researchers shouldn't try to build theories based on accurate assumptions about human behavior; that, on the contrary, their ability to understand the social world should increase insofar as they worked with incorrect assumptions. As he put it:

> Truly important and significant hypotheses will be found
> to have "assumptions" that are widely inaccurate descriptive

representations of reality, and, in general, the more significant the theory, the more unrealistic the assumptions . . . The reason is simple. A hypothesis is important if it "explains" much by little, that is, if it abstracts the common and crucial elements from the mass of complex and detailed circumstances surrounding the phenomenon to be explained and permits valid predictions on the basis of them alone. To be important, therefore, a hypothesis must be descriptively false in its assumptions.[16]

Friedman was defending the use of the rationality assumption in economics, and it seems to me he was both right and wrong. It is certainly the case that all of science works by simplifying its models of the world. We understand the motions of the planets by treating them as perfect spheres, or even as objects with all their mass concentrated at a single point, and generally ignore everything else—their distortions in shape, the gases that swirl in their atmospheres, and so on. We ignore most details, and this is okay because our models do include the most important details about the distribution of the mass of a planet, which determines how it moves in a gravitational field, and also how it exerts gravitational forces on other planets. Models of planetary motion are indeed "descriptively false" in their assumptions, but their power derives from the very core of what they get right.

Undoubtedly, the science of man must similarly be built upon a simplified picture of individuals and what drives them. But a simplified picture can get the nub of human behavior right or wrong. It can throw out only the unimportant details, or it can throw out some of the most important ones too. This is where Friedman's argument goes wrong, and where "rational" economics falls down. The rationality assumption doesn't give only an incomplete description of human behavior, but a fundamentally distorted one; it presupposes that people do not learn, that they do not formulate hypotheses and test them, that they never change their minds. In effect, it wipes most of real-world human behavior out of existence. The picture of human behavior as fundamentally adaptive is just as simple, conceptually, as the rational view, yet it accords with reality—especially for people making decisions in the uncertain and ever-changing setting of a market.

What sets this modern thinking apart from long tradition is the belief that it is not individual human complexity that makes markets hard to understand, but the delicate order and organization among the many people within any market. It is, again, pattern rather than people. For the orthodox traditionalists in many economics departments, this may be a little too much to swallow. Yet it is the success of these ideas that explains why Oxford University recently selected a young physicist, Neil Johnson, rather than any esteemed professor of economics or finance, to head up its new Department of Computational Finance. Johnson and a handful of other physicists have proven the power of this approach in the most dramatic way possible—by showing how it is possible, at least in some cases, to predict the financial future.

SEEING THE FUTURE

Nothing gets more attention from the business and financial press than predictions about market winners and losers, who's hot and who's not, which stock is a certain moneymaker, and which a dead loss. There's always a "guru" getting press attention for his or her supposed insight into market trends, even while numerous empirical studies suggest that virtually no scheme for making financial predictions has ever been successful, except temporarily, or by luck.[17] Academic studies generally support the view, expressed by the late economist John Kenneth Galbraith, that the economic system survives "not because of the excellence of the work of those who forecast its future, but because of their supremely reliable commitment to error."[18]

It could be, of course, that the economic system, and markets in particular, are just inherently unpredictable. Or maybe it is that science just hasn't yet advanced to a level of sophistication at which prediction would become possible. The numbers streaming across a computer on Neil Johnson's desk suggest the latter interpretation. The numbers reflect the ups and downs of the foreign exchange rate between the U.S. dollar and the Japanese yen. Just before each new price appears, his computer predicts whether the rate will go up or down from its last value. It is getting the answer right most of the time. The secret? A deep understanding of the physics of markets, which Johnson has parlayed into a powerful tool for detecting patterns that no one else can see.

Johnson's technique grew out of some brilliant work of the late 1990s by physicists Yi-Cheng Zhang and Damien Challet, then both at the University of Fribourg in Switzerland, who tried to pare Arthur's model of the El Farol bar down to its simplest possible terms. In their Minority Game, you have a crowd of people, and in each round, each person has to choose either 0 or 1. The goal is to be in the minority—to choose what most others don't choose. This is almost exactly the same as Arthur's game, only the logic is made as spare as possible. Players in the Minority Game look to the recent history of outcomes—the record of whether more people chose 0 or 1 in each round—and use this history to make predictions for the future and to guide their own behavior. What makes this simplification valuable is that Zhang and Challet were able to work out the behavior of their game not only with the computer, but analytically—with pencil and paper. They uncovered a beautiful surprise.

Their results show that in the Minority Game—and by implication, in the El Farol game, or in any of the adaptive market models based around it—things should work very differently depending on the number of people who participate. When few people take part, they found, the limited number of strategies in play isn't enough to cover the space of possible patterns. If there is some meaningful pattern linking past outcomes with future outcomes, the players will try to learn it and use it to their advantage. But if the particular pattern lies in one of the group's "blind spots"—that is, no particular player has this pattern in his repertoire of strategies—then no one can exploit it. Consequently, the pattern will persist and never get washed away. In contrast, if enough players participate, their strategies will cover all possibilities. Any pattern in the sequence of outcomes will be noticed and jumped on immediately. In the former case, the collective outcome (or the movement of the price in the market) will follow predictable patterns. In the latter, all predictable patterns should dissolve into unpredictable randomness. Surprisingly, Challet and Zhang showed that the transition from one regime into the other works much like a "phase transition" in physics, as when solid ice melts into liquid water.

This transition from a predictable regime into an unpredictable regime may seem somewhat esoteric, but it may also have a lot to do with explaining why real markets are so hard to predict, yet why so many people continue to try. Think about it. Suppose there aren't enough people in the market, so the collection of strategies in play isn't enough to cover all possibilities. There will then be some residual "predictability" in the market, which will naturally entice other people to enter, as they can earn an easy profit. Further people may enter for the same reason. But each new player who enters, by bringing more strategies into play, effectively "eats up" part of that residual predictability. People will continue to enter only to the point where the predictability gets washed away entirely, and the market becomes completely unpredictable. At this point, of course, some people, unable any longer to profit, may decide to leave the market—taking their strategies with them and bringing a tiny bit of predictability back again. By this argument, the market should hover near the boundary of predictability, where limited prediction is possible, but difficult.

It is hard to know for sure if this picture represents the truth about real markets. But the idea is so elegant and appealing, it seems so right, that in 1998, when Johnson first heard it, an intriguing possibility entered his head. If markets do, at least sometimes, possess a degree of predictability, it should be possible to detect it. Although Zhang and Challet's game is obviously far simpler than any real market, it captures the basic logic of what drives the market—the underlying ecology of strategies among the investors—in at least a rudimentary way. Moreover, its natural internal structure is certainly richer and more complex than most of the mathematical schemes that real investors use to predict the market. Hence, he reasoned, it might be the perfect tool—or at least better than anything else currently available—for identifying whatever limited degree of predictability might reside in the market's behavior. Working with colleagues at Oxford, he was soon able to turn this idea into a practical technique—one that really works.

To get things going in any Minority Game (or in any of the virtual markets based around it), at the outset researchers have to assign some set of "theories" to the players, the ideas they will hold in their heads as possibilities for predicting the world. By choosing the initial strategies carefully, Johnson and colleagues were able to "tune" their market until it reproduced some particular pattern of price movements, say those observed recently in the New York Stock Exchange. Through such tuning, they hoped, the ecology of theories in the heads of the agents in the model might come to have some rough correspondence with the real ecology of ideas and beliefs in the heads of real investors. It is the detailed structure of this ecology that drives market movements. Hence, by running the model forward into the future, they suspected, you might be able to predict where the real market is going.

It makes intuitive sense, and, more important, good predictions. In a number of tests, Johnson and colleagues have found that their model can first detect certain moments when the market is more predictable than others. These are the moments when the number of strategies in play has effectively been reduced, either because people have dropped out of the market, or many have begun using the same strategy. Johnson calls these moments "pockets of predictability." The computer can not only recognize these, but can then predict what will come next. In a recent demonstration using data on the U.S. dollar versus the Japanese yen, Johnson's group was able to identify roughly ninety good pockets of prediction in a series of four thousand consecutive prices.[19] The model then predicted the direction of the price movement correctly for all of these, with only one error. Of course, if success in this regard becomes routine, the implications may be a little bizarre. The method would surely be adopted by many large investors, which would change the nature and philosophy of the markets themselves and perhaps undermine the technique's ability to make predictions. It's also possible that those predictions might be self-fulfilling. If the model predicted an imminent 5 percent jump in the New York Stock Exchange, investors armed with this knowledge would naturally flock to the market, buying stocks to make a profit and thereby driving prices up—probably by about 5 percent.

THE ROAD TO REALITY

In this chapter I've looked exclusively at financial markets. This is obviously a rather narrow and specialized slice of the human social world, but represents a natural starting point as the one domain where a form of collective human activity has been closely scrutinized in mathematical terms. It is also the part of human life where one might expect us to be at our most rational and calculating, and where the orthodox view of economic theory might stand the best chance of getting things right. In this narrow setting, however, for over forty years the puzzle of "fat tails" has cried out for explanation. Why are markets of all kinds inherently unruly? Remarkably, we've found that the answer emerges not by looking into the deep complexity of individuals, into the sophistication of their thoughts and their weird habits, but to the simplicity of their behavior. We've seen in this one setting how a retreat to simple rules can lead to an impressive improvement in understanding. The fat tails that took down LTCM are no longer a mystery; in the most recent laws for international banking and risk assessment, they are now being taken into account.

Market models based around adaptive agents are also becoming powerful tools not only for predicting markets, but for predicting what might happen to markets under unusual conditions. Companies have saved themselves lots of money by using them.

Several years ago, for example, executives of the NASDAQ stock exchange planned to change the tick size—the basic price increment—of its securities listings and switch to decimalization from prices listed in fractions. They expected this would make it easier for the market to discover the accurate price of stocks, because traders could express their market views more precisely. The result would be a smaller difference between the "bid" and "ask" prices (at which traders are willing to buy and sell securities), attracting more investors and companies to their exchange. It sounded like an obviously good idea, but the exchange wisely decided to investigate further before going ahead. They developed a model of their exchange based around adaptive agents of the type found in the Minority Game, or in Johnson's market models. Importantly, the agents were able to adapt and alter their strategies on the fly, or even discover new strategies, as they identified trends or patterns in the market. Once the model was working like the real market—reproducing price fluctuations in a mathematically accurate way—the company could use it as a laboratory. Surprisingly, they found that reducing the tick size beyond a certain point actually increased the bid–ask spread. As it turned out, agents learned how to exploit some tricky strategies that made quick profits for them at the expense of overall market efficiency. These strategies grew less risky and more profitable with a smaller tick size, and their use spoiled the benefits that NASDAQ had expected. Fortunately, however, they discovered this before learning the same lesson in reality. When the exchange went ahead with its plans and actually changed the tick size from $\frac{1}{16}$ to $\frac{1}{100}$ in 2001, it was able to anticipate this effect and take steps to counteract it.[20]

All this has become possible by taking a more simple-minded approach to human behavior. We all simplify the world and form hypotheses about how it works. We keep ideas that seem to work and ditch those that do not. Adaptation of this kind is perhaps our greatest talent. In another context, for example, it is obvious that none of us learns to speak and communicate by rational contemplation. Nor do we gain this capacity solely by virtue of some special language "organ" tucked away in the brain that gives us "hardwired" ability. The more linguists learn about language and how we use it, in fact, the more they see our skills as adaptive creatures as absolutely fundamental. Two people come to a conversation. Normally we think that they arrive with their languages fixed and unchangeable. But research over the past decade or so suggests otherwise, that the patterns of speech, the words used, the style of pronunciation, all vary slightly, even in a single conversation, depending on how that conversation evolves, on the give-and-take between the two parties. Language isn't fixed and static, but an ongoing evolutionary process, not unlike the ever-shifting ecology of ideas and beliefs in any market, all made possible—perhaps inevitable—by our adaptive capacity.

Again, to understand things correctly, we must learn to think in terms of patterns, rather than people. Indeed, at Sony Laboratories in Paris, computer scientist Luc Steels has shown that even extremely unintelligent robots can, just by adaptation, learn to invent and negotiate shared languages, starting from scratch. They start by inventing random words as names for objects in their environments (akin to the random strategies in Arthur's El Farol). They try these words out and see how they work, keeping those that lead to successful communication, and forgetting those that do not. Through a simple process of repetitive comparison, learning from one another, even these robots can quickly build up a shared language—not only shared words, but grammatical structures as well.[21]

Adaptation is powerful. But there is more to the social atom, of course, than adaptive thinking. Man is rightly known as the social animal, for as individuals we are more strongly entwined with one another's lives than the members of any other species. If we imagine the social atom in splendid isolation, facing problems as an individual, then thinking about our adaptive qualities, in addition to our talent for rational calculation, might be enough. But going further means looking at how social atoms interact, in pairs and in groups, how their actions affect one another. As a first step, it means recognizing that when any two or more people get together, or even when they don't, but have some means of learning about what each other has done, one thing is sure to follow—imitation. In addition to being flexible adapters, we're born imitators.

Chapter 5

THE IMITATING ATOM

*The average man is destitute of independence of opin-
ion. He is not interested in contriving an opinion of
his own, by study and reflection, but is only anxious
to find out what his neighbor's opinion is and slav-
ishly adopt it.*

— MARK TWAIN

ACCORDING TO THE *Roanoke Times*, this is what happened in southern Virginia in the winter of 1933–34. One
quiet evening in December, a Mrs. Cal Huffman of Roanoke
saw a mysterious man lurking on her farm and, soon afterward,
smelled gas. Thirty minutes later, her husband also smelled gas
and called the police. The authorities came to the property, but
found nothing unusual. Nevertheless, news of what had happened traveled, and five days later, a Mr. and Mrs. Clarence Hall,
living in a village nearby, came home from church to a sickening
smell. Whatever it was made their eyes burn, and a neighbor told
police she had seen a man shining a flashlight into one of the
Halls' windows. Two weeks later, when a Mrs. Moore of nearby
Howell's Mill heard muffled voices in her yard and then also

smelled gas, a *Roanoke Times* headline announced that a deranged maniac seemed to be attacking people in the area.

The mystery of the Virginia gas attacks grew more puzzling as months went by. People in and around Roanoke kept their doors locked at all times and scanned surrounding fields eagerly for strange figures, especially at dusk. People sat on their porches with guns. In one incident, a man ran outside after smelling gas in his house and fired a shotgun at four men heading into the woods. But by this time the police were beginning to wonder. In all of the twenty or thirty reported attacks, investigating officers had found no physical evidence of gas—no canisters, for example, or soaked rags. What they had found were, among other things, an idling car with a faulty exhaust, coal fumes issuing from a stove, and volatile chemicals evaporating from a radiator. On February 14, 1934, the *Roanoke Times* published an article under the headline "Roanoke Has No Gasser," after which there were no more attacks. The entire episode, police concluded, was the product of "overwrought minds"—and the power of one mind to plant seeds of interpretation into another.[1]

Everyone knows plenty of stories of rumors taking on a life of their own and becoming "established fact" without even a shred of real evidence. People in the 1930s, of course, were no more suggestible than we are today. In August 2005, in the devastating aftermath of Hurricane Katrina, terrifying reports began trickling out of New Orleans about roaming gangs setting upon helpless tourists, killing men and raping women. Fox News (or Faux News, as some bloggers on the Web refer to it) issued an "alert" about rampant "robberies, rapes, carjackings, and riots," and "little babies" being raped at the Superdome. Yet reporters and officials several weeks later were still struggling to find any of the victims of these alleged crimes. "We have no official reports to document any murder," the police superintendent then noted. The stories were, almost without exception, mere rumors.

Rumors and episodes of mass panic illustrate what seems to be a pervasive tendency among human beings to copy the behavior of others. It was not rational, considered action that led to the Hula Hoop craze of the late 1950s, the Beanie Babies mania of the 1990s, or the body-piercing frenzy of today. Few would say it was the full glory of independent human intelligence that led one Dutchman, during the tulip mania of the 1630s, to purchase a single bulb at the expense of one thousand pounds of cheese, two tons of butter, four tons of beer, twelve sheep, eight pigs, four oxen, and other valuable goods, including a silver drinking cup.[2] As a more frightening example of the power of imitation, consider the riots that engulfed Paris and other parts of France in October 2005. On October 27, Bouna Traore and Zyed Benna, two teenage boys, died after being chased by police in Clichy-sous-Bois, a Parisian suburb. The boys (who were innocent) were electrocuted while hiding in an electrical substation. Over the next two weeks, almost three thousand people were arrested as a wave of civic violence leapt from Paris to other cities in France—to Lyon, Dijon, and Évreux—as if social sparks were drifting in the wind and igniting new fires elsewhere. A fifteen-year-old boy, a participant in the riots, summed up the strangely contagious spirit in an interview with the *New York Times*. At first, he said, the two boys being killed "was a good excuse" for rioting. But now it was different: "It's fun to set cars on fire."

Why are humans as a species so susceptible to self-propelling waves of mass behavior? Last chapter we met rule number one for the social atom: We're highly skilled at recognizing patterns and adapting to a changing world. We interact with the world and learn from it. But we also learn, or try to learn, from others.

We live our lives within families and networks of friends, with colleagues and neighbors, and amid a cacophony of voices and opinions blasted out from television, newspapers, and the Web. Far from being isolated, like atoms in a perfect vacuum, we are fully interdependent and embedded in a thick social tapestry of others, like atoms in a dense liquid, where we can barely move without jostling against others. Our social "embeddedness" influences what we wear and eat, the work we do, our opinions and thoughts.[3] We do not think entirely on our own—what we believe and why depends strongly on our interactions with others.

In this chapter, we'll explore another aspect of the social atom, a behavioral habit that applies whenever two or more social atoms get together. Next to our ability to adapt, perhaps nothing is so pronounced in human behavior as our capacity for imitation. Infants learn within a few minutes to imitate their parents' facial expressions. The Romans, well aware of our imitating tendencies, hired professional mourners to kick off the wailing at important funerals.[4] We have hardwired instincts for imitation, yet often we also imitate consciously, as imitation offers a strategy, often our only strategy, for taking advantage of things that others may have learned. Of course, imitation can lead to weird and costly distortions, because those others don't always know very much. But ultimately, the surprising influence of imitation needn't be mysterious or puzzling—scientists are finding that it often leads to patterns as regular as clockwork.

SEEING IS BELIEVING

In 1952, a handful of volunteers came to a laboratory on the campus of Swarthmore College, near Philadelphia, to take part in a study of human perception. Social psychologist Solomon Asch had a simple plan. He had two large cards, one with a single vertical line drawn on it, and the other with three similar lines. The volunteers, after looking at both cards, were to say which of the three lines had the same length as the single line. Asch had given two of the lines different lengths; different enough so that any child could get the right answer. But he also had a trick up his sleeve.

Some of the "volunteers" weren't actually volunteers at all, but were in cahoots with Asch as part of the experiment. In the experimental trials, he arranged it so that a string of these fake volunteers would give their answers, out loud, before the real experimental subject had to give his or her answer. Sometimes Asch had his accomplices all give the same wrong answer, to see if this might affect the real subject. The results were astonishing. When doing the test on their own, as a control, none of the subjects ever gave a wrong answer. They could easily tell the lines apart. But when they heard the others give the same wrong answer, the subjects often followed along, also giving the same wrong answer as the majority. They hesitated, smiled uncomfortably, rubbed their eyes and squinted at the cards, then went with the crowd over their own perceptions. The mere verbal reports of a number of others were enough to coerce otherwise independent minds into seeing—or at least saying they had seen—something that wasn't there.[5]

It is a commonplace observation that people tend to "go along with the crowd." Some of those in Asch's experiments may have gone along from a lack of self-confidence, doubting their own perceptions after seeing others, in numbers, choose differently. Whatever the explanation, Asch found the results disturbing: "That we have found the tendency to conformity in our society so strong that reasonably intelligent and well-meaning young people are willing to call White Black is a matter of concern. It raises questions about our ways of education and about the values that guide our conduct."[6]

Writing during the McCarthy era, amid the unthinking hysteria of his communist witch hunt, Asch had good reason to be concerned about education and values. But it now appears that our conformist tendencies may, in fact, have much deeper biological roots.

Two years ago, a team of researchers led by neuroscientist Gregory Burns of Emery University in Atlanta took Asch's experiment a step further, using MRI to monitor the brain activity of subjects facing similar situations. They had volunteers look at pictures of two apparently different three-dimensional shapes. They were then to say if the two objects were really different, or if they were only views of the same object from different angles. Answering required some mental rearrangement and rotation of the objects. As in Asch's experiments, Burns and colleagues arranged for some actors to pretend to be other volunteers, and sometimes to give the wrong answers. On their own, subjects always gave the right answers. When the actors intervened, however, subjects caved in about 40 percent of the time, abandoning their own minds for the majority's.[7]

Even more interesting, however, is what the MRI showed going on in the subjects' brains when they faced the challenge of breaking with the group opinion. If they were making their decisions consciously—perceiving the lines correctly, but then choosing to go along with the group—you would expect to see lots of brain activity in the forebrain, a region generally involved in planning and solving problems. But this isn't what Burns and his colleagues found. Instead, when people followed the majority, against their own view, brain activity was highest in the right intraparietal sulcus, a brain area devoted to spatial awareness and perception. This suggests that individuals weren't only deciding, after deliberation, to go along with the group, but were actually seeing the objects differently. What the others reported actually influenced what they saw. As the authors put it, "The social setting alters the individual's perception of the world." Burns and colleagues also found that on occasions when people successfully resisted the group pressure, brain activity took place mainly in regions associated with emotion, as if they instinctively felt risk in breaking with the group.

These experiments suggest that the roots of imitative behavior are in some cases quite archaic indeed. It seems to be automatic, unconscious, and instinctual, hardwired into our biological makeup. We might call this "deep" imitation, as it has deep psychic roots that reflect our evolutionary history. But there is a shallower kind of imitation, perhaps even more influential, based around a conscious strategy for making decisions. "One of man's advantages over the lower animals," as Aristotle suggested long ago, "is that he is the most imitative creature in the world." We're good adapters. And one of the things we adapt to most frequently is other people.

Thinking like Penguins

Collectively, penguins face a daily dilemma. They survive on a steady diet of fish taken from the icy blue sea. But there's more beneath the surface than fish. Violent death sometimes lurks there as well, in the form of killer whales, and so penguins have to be cautious, entering the water only when they know it is safe. This is where things get tricky. If a killer whale stays below the surface, a penguin on land cannot know it is there. The only way

to find out is to take the plunge or wait and hope that some
other more reckless penguin will get tired of waiting and jump
in. So penguins, especially at the beginning of each day, play a
waiting game akin to killer-whale roulette. They stand around
for hours until finally some desperate penguin jumps in, at which
point it is then all or nothing for the entire group. A bloodbath,
and everyone stays put; if things go all right, everyone dives in to
look for a meal. (As it turns out, some penguins try to help things
along by giving their neighbors the occasional not-so-gentle
nudge.)[8]

We generally go about our lives thinking that we make up our
own mind. But we're actually a lot like penguins—when information is scarce, we gather whatever fragments we can by watching
others. Few of us would choose an empty restaurant over one
packed with people; we suspect they must be there for a reason.
Banks open new branches in locations where they see that other
banks have branches, and business analysts know that smaller companies tend to copy the behavior of larger companies. If a leader
such as Intel invests in some radical new technology for making
computer chips, smaller firms will do the same, guessing that Intel,
with its vast resources, probably knows what it is doing. Imitation
can be a legitimate strategy that helps both the individual and the
group. It is a form of what biologists call social learning—learning
by interaction with others, rather than by oneself—and it makes
us, in many cases, a lot smarter than we would be on our own. Our
instinct for imitation is so deep that it is difficult, if you see twenty
people staring into the sky, not to look up yourself. But social imitation, for all its information-gathering benefits, also routinely
leads people off the path of good sense.

In October 2002, a mysterious assassin began shooting people
at random in the Washington, D.C., area. On October 3, the killer

struck five times in fifteen hours, killing a landscaper cutting grass, a taxi driver pumping gasoline, and a woman reading a book on a park bench, among others. Police heard two reports of a white van seen near the crimes, so they set up roadblocks and searched any van or truck of the right color. Newspapers and television and radio stations repeated the white van leads, and soon everyone "knew" what the killer was driving. That's how things stayed for two weeks. But then the police, quite by chance while following another lead, checked the license plate of a blue Chevrolet Caprice sedan registered to someone on a list of potential suspects. Surprised, and probably more than a little embarrassed, they discovered that this blue Caprice had actually been stopped by police near several of the shootings, but let go each time—largely because the car wasn't a white van. Within hours of publicizing the blue Caprice lead, and following tips from alert citizens, police arrested John Allen Muhammad, forty-one, and John Lee Malvo, seventeen, at a rest area along a highway in Maryland.

The problem is obvious. Imitation doesn't generate any new information, it only amplifies the consequences that a little bit of information can have, whether it is real information or not. In 1995, when two writers on management theory, Michael Treacy and Fred Wiersema, published a book entitled *The Discipline of the Market Leaders*, they bought up fifty thousand copies of their own book, especially from bookstores where sales were monitored to determine the *New York Times*' best-sellers lists. Even though the book had only mediocre reviews, it shot right onto the list. What's more, being there was enough to generate further sales that kept it there.[9]

These examples illustrate the spectacular surprises made possible merely by one person influencing another. We may imitate blindly, following a social instinct, or strategically, because we think someone knows more than we do. In other cases, as we'll see shortly, the actions of others can even coerce us into going along by making imitation our obvious best strategy. Whatever its origin, however, one thing about imitation is that it makes it hard to trace the path between social cause and effect, as the actions of a few can rapidly transform the world of the many. This is one of the reasons social science has always had such difficulty in moving past "storytelling" to find deeper, "lawlike" explanations of events. Of course, imitation doesn't really sever the link between cause and effect, it only seems that way. It's not so hard, if we focus on patterns rather than people, to get a better picture of how it works.

MECHANICAL MAN

For the most part, economic theorists have generally tried to ignore the influence of human imitation altogether. An idea still prominent in economists' theories is the "representative agent," which says that if something happens and you want to know how a group of people will respond to it—think of the riots in Paris, for example—you can totally ignore the interactions between people. Every person will look to what happened and decide independently whether to riot. If 2 percent do riot, in this view, it's because the event was sufficiently "emotive" or influential to cause 2 percent to take action. The idea is that you can think of the crowd itself as having a "character" that reflects the average character of the people that make it up. This way of thinking implies, clearly, that outcomes should always be in proportion to the events that trigger them; tiny causes should never have enormous repercussions.

This idea is great if you want to keep your mathematics easy, work out theories in tidy equations, and achieve the illusion of certainty. But it's not so good if you want to explain the real world, because it ignores people like that boy who discovered that "it's fun to set cars on fire." What the representative-agent idea misses is that what gets a riot going, at the outset, isn't necessarily the same as what keeps it going or determines how big it eventually gets. The first person to start a riot does it all on his or her own; but after 100 people have begun smashing things up, the decision for the 101st is completely different. It is not nearly so hard to join in when everyone you know is doing it. Many crimes do really seem to work this way. In an important study of ten years ago, for example, Harvard economists Edward Glaeser, Bruce Sacerdote, and Jose Schienkman found that the difference in crime rates from place to place, between cities, or even between different parts of a city cannot be explained just by referring to the differing economic conditions in those places. Quite simply, crime rates vary far more wildly from place to place than economic conditions do. However, the variation can be explained if one assumes that the presence of some criminals in an area makes it more likely that other people there will become criminals. They found that the effect is particularly strong for crimes such as larceny and auto theft, significant for crimes such as assault, burglary, and robbery, yet weaker for crimes such as arson and murder.[10]

In 1978, Stanford University sociologist Mark Granovetter pioneered a clever way to come to grips with the delicacy of such situations. Stimulated by Thomas Schelling's "atomic physics" approach to social science, Granovetter tried to boil things down to utter simplicity. Think again of the rioting example. Most of us wouldn't start a riot over nothing, but Granovetter supposed that we might join in under the right circumstances—if we were, in some sense, "pushed" far enough. That is, we all have some "threshold" for joining a riot. One person might join a riot if ten others were already smashing things up, whereas another might join only when there were sixty or seventy. The level of someone's threshold might depend on all kinds of things—personality, threats of punishment, and so on. Some might not riot under any conditions, while a rare few might readily kick things off themselves.

Logically speaking, in any specific situation, we all must have some threshold, although it may be rather difficult to determine in practice. A person's threshold reflects the point, as Granovetter put it, "where the perceived benefits to an individual of doing the thing in question (here, joining the riot) exceed the perceived costs." What is important is that the balance between benefits and costs often depends not only on our own individual preferences, but on what other people are doing, and how many of them are doing it. The mere existence of such thresholds, reflecting the power of interpersonal influence over behavior, can make a group's behavior extremely difficult to predict.

For example, imagine that one hundred people have thresholds ranging from 0 to 99. One person has threshold 0, another 1, another 2, and so on. In this case, a large riot will be inevitable. The "radical" with threshold 0 will kick it off, then to be joined by the person with threshold 1, and the riot will grow, eventually involving even the "high threshold" people. But notice how delicately the outcome depends on the precise interlocking of these thresholds. Remove the person with threshold 1, and after the first person starts smashing things up, the rest would simply stand by watching. With no one willing to be the second person into the riot, there would be no chain reaction. So a tiny difference in the character of just one person can have a dramatic effect on the overall group. As Granovetter noted, however, a storytelling explanation would miss this subtlety and make the representative-agent mistake of attributing the outcome to the "character" of the crowd. In the former case, the story might say "a crowd of radicals engaged in riotous behavior," while in the latter it might instead report "a demented troublemaker broke a window while a group of solid citizens looked on."[11]

The "atomic physics" of social cascades suggests that there is no easy way around this problem, whether you're talking about a riot, a wave of pessimism washing over a housing market, or a vote being taken at some board meeting. Accurate and detailed predictions should almost be out of the question, as any tiny detail can intrude on the larger picture. Tiny differences in a crowd, the presence or absence of a few people of the right type, might be the difference between a couple of broken windows and entire blocks in flame. The outcome of a vote may depend entirely on the order in which the people voted. (Curiously, but perhaps quite wisely, judges in U.S. navy courts-martial vote in inverse order of rank to minimize the influence of imitation.)

This way of looking at things seems likely to be the real key to what happened in Times Square, for it reveals how a social situation can easily have two stable conditions, possibly very different, and how things can flip from one to the other quite suddenly. In 1995, it was obvious to any company that the Times Square area had great potential; the risks were also obvious, given the area's long economic decline. Potential investors had to feel a lot like penguins standing around a hole in the ice in the moments before anyone has jumped in. After Disney did jump in, committing themselves to renovating the New Amsterdam Theatre, executives at companies like Madame Tussaud's Wax Museum and entertainment conglomerate AMC could feel safety in numbers: a bad decision doesn't look nearly so bad if others make it too. Something else was at work in this case too—positive feedback. For those executives, going along with the crowd was not only psychologically safe; it also made legitimate sense because the participation of others made the area more attractive. In real terms, Times Square became more attractive as more investors jumped in, improving the local economy, which then in turn attracted more investors. This example captures the logic of Granovetter's analysis of rioting almost perfectly.

Though seemingly quite different, the "miracle" of Kerala that I mentioned earlier also seems to offer an example of the same thing—a dramatic social cascade driven by a behavior that becomes more attractive the more people do it. Learning to read and write isn't so important in a rural community where few others read and write, and where life revolves around traditional agricultural production. It is not hard to see why few parents would encourage education for their children, seeing no likely benefit from it. Things could stay that way for a long time; in Kerala, in fact, they did. But everything becomes different in a community where most people read and write, and where economic life revolves around manufacturing and a bustling retail trade, where managerial skills are important. The education of children now becomes essential to their success, and a keen desire of every parent. If Times Square made the transition through the first step of one influential company, Kerala went from a low to high level of education through the concerted effort of an organized army of volunteers. Through their efforts, in effect, the state crossed over a barrier and now lies on the other side. Education has entrained individuals into a new, self-sustaining social pattern.

Granovetter's way of thinking makes it clear that understanding the consequences of interpersonal influence is tricky indeed.

Yet it also suggests that the workings of social transformations driven by such influences may not be completely beyond mathematical science. Researchers have recently taken Granovetter's ideas further. In so doing, they've found that the flip side of contingency is a surprisingly universal law—a striking example of the hidden physics of the social world.

THE PHYSICS OF OPINION

French physicist Jean-Philippe Bouchaud has a rather unusual résumé. Aside from his experience in core areas of physics—in the physics of "spin glasses" and granular matter—Bouchaud has been a pioneer in the rapidly emerging subfield known as econophysics, which uses mathematical ideas inspired by physics to tackle problems in economics and finance. Fifteen years ago, Bouchaud and a team of physicists even started their own hedge fund—Capital Fund Management—which uses the physics-based understanding of markets and market fluctuations to manage money. Several years ago, when Bouchaud learned about Granovetter's "threshold" models of human imitation, he immediately noticed an almost incredible coincidence—that the way people influence one another in Granovetter's picture turns out to be virtually identical, mathematically, to the way atoms do in some of physicists' most elegant theories. Prying into this weird connection in greater detail, Bouchaud, along with colleague Quentin Michard, found a way to build similar theories for people.

The physics in question describes how atoms interact within a piece of magnetic material such as iron. In such a substance, the atoms are like microscopic magnets, with north and south poles; you can think of them as tiny arrows pointing in various directions. Put the chunk of iron in a strong magnetic field, and all

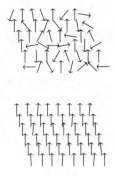

Figure 7

the tiny arrows will tend to line up with it, like soldiers falling into formation. But even in the absence of such an overwhelming external force, these atoms also influence each other; if many point in one direction, they tend to coerce others nearby to line up in the same way also (see figure 7). This logic, Bouchaud realized, is much like Granovetter's take on the social world. We all respond to external influences—the social norm that favors peaceful behavior over violence, for example. But we're also influenced, often even more strongly, by each other.

So if you think, abstractly, of the direction of an atom within a magnet as an "opinion" or "behavior," you can think of what's happening at the atomic level as imitation—what one atom does influences what others might do. On the face of it, this may seem like nothing more than a forced and rather sterile analogy. But it turns out to be much more.

First, the physics. Suppose you start with the magnetic field pointing downward. It is strong enough so that it coerces all the tiny atomic magnets also to point downward. Now suppose that you gradually change the direction of the field so that it slowly rotates from being downward to being upward. As it does, it will influence the atoms. Some will begin to flip from pointing down to pointing up. If they didn't influence one another, the entire change would be gradual—more and more atoms would flip, one by one, until they all came to be pointing upward, obeying the external influence of the magnetic field. But the influence of one atom on another makes the change take place in a very different way—both faster and less smoothly. In real experiments, you find that one atom flipping can push others nearby over the edge, making them flip too, which then can trigger others. So the transition from everyone pointing down to everyone pointing up happens in an erratic way, as a series of smaller and larger avalanches, rather than all gradually. In addition, the entire crowd of atoms comes to be pointing upward far sooner than it would without influences between atoms. The speed of the change is amplified.

What does this have to do with the social world? Following Bouchaud and Michard, think of the external magnetic field as some set of outside factors or circumstances that influence human behavior. Take mobile phones, for example. When mobile phones first came onto the market, they were bulky and expensive, more difficult to use than ordinary telephones in the home. Not surprisingly, not many people were persuaded to buy them. Twenty years later, everything has changed; mobile phones are cheap and useful and almost everyone now has one. You can think of this change over twenty years as being analogous to that field swinging from one direction to another, and coercing the atomic magnets to come along with it. In this case, technological changes coerced changes in people's behavior. Remarkably, as Bouchaud and Michard have demonstrated, this analogy holds in more than qualitative terms. Analyzing data for cell-phone adoption during the 1990s, they found that the rate of adoption precisely follows the mathematical pattern predicted by the magnetic model. The implication in this case is not entirely surprising: many people were buying phones not because they had decided based on real information about how much they would benefit, but because their friends and colleagues were buying them.

Now most of us can probably accept that imitation influences our behavior when we're choosing a movie or a car, buying cell phones, or shopping for clothes. We are far less likely to admit that imitation has a strong influence over the more "important" elements of our lives—say, in the kind of work we do, our political or religious views, or in our decisions to have children. Here we are at our most independent—or so we like to think. But perhaps we have to think again. Bouchaud and Michard looked at the data for the dramatically falling European birthrates between the years 1950 and 2000. Undoubtedly, many real underlying factors were behind this trend, such as changing economic conditions, more career opportunities for women, and so on. But the data say that these factors account for only a fraction of the change. The two physicists found that birthrates changed far too fast to be explained by independent decision making based on external factors alone. Many people had to be making decisions not to have children, or to have fewer children, by imitation rather than by independent judgment. "The natural trend," the physicists concluded, "was substantially amplified and exaggerated by peer pressure."[12]

One of the more paradoxical lessons of this work, it seems to me, is what it says about the social transformations that surprise us the most. In further mathematical analysis, Bouchaud and Michard found that when the influence of one person on another is sufficiently strong, one should in fact expect social changes to take place not just rapidly but discontinuously—with a large fraction of the population changing from one behavior or opinion to another at almost precisely the same moment. When the real underlying factors affecting people's decisions are weak, such transformations should literally seem to come out of the blue—as if caused by nothing at all. This suggests that what we find most unsettling about situations such as the renewal of Times Square or the cultural transformation of Kerala—that things might easily have remained as they were, possibly for a long time—may really be true. In effect, the most dramatic and puzzling social transformations may in fact lack any clear under-lying cause and simply reflect the possible flipping of a group's collective behavior from one stable state to another. In some ways, this is a disappointing answer, as it says that there is no "deeper" answer, yet it makes sense of a fundamental puzzle of social theory itself—why many important events seem to lack any sensible basis in simple cause and effect.

One slightly spooky addendum to the story. As an amusing aside, the two physicists tested their model to see how well it predicts the way episodes of clapping begin, and then abruptly end, following a concert. You know, a few people start it off, everyone then joins in, and then, finally, the clapping tapers off, with a few late clappers, and then silence. Not surprisingly, the model works beautifully in this case, as this phenomenon is driven almost entirely by imitation—indeed, the only goal is to clap when others are clapping, and to stop when they do. But this means that if you put the data for clapping—recorded from various concerts—next to the data for birthrates and cell phones, and correct them for the natural but unimportant difference in timescales, you find that all three phenomena fall onto precisely the same mathematical curve (see figure 8). Despite our free will, and despite the vast differences between deciding to clap or have a child, the way others' actions influence our own decisions leads to a universal pattern.

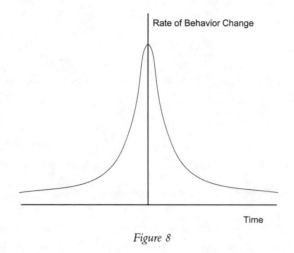

Figure 8

It's a little unnerving to think that in our larger life, in the really big decisions we make, on having children, taking one kind of job over another, we might be responding to forces—social forces— that are utterly identical in form and influence to those that control our clapping at the end of a concert. But we're social beings through and through, embedded in the crowd and not distinct from it. We're not as free as our vanity would have us believe.

KEEPING IT SIMPLE

Good science thrives on judicious approximation. There is no such thing as a "perfect" or "complete" model of anything. Only by ignoring parts of any picture can we answer questions that matter to us. Why is copper a good conductor of electricity? Physicists know that the gravitational force makes every electron, proton, and neutron in a piece of solid copper tug on every other such particle. They also know, however, that these forces are so unbelievably weak that they cannot possibly have anything to do with why copper atoms fall into neat crystalline structures through which electricity moves so easily. The one key point that cannot be ignored is that, when copper atoms get together, one electron from each slips away from its host and is able to move through the material quite easily.

Explaining anything means focusing on the details that matter, and ignoring those that do not, and we have to approach the social atom and the world made of social atoms in the same way. It is not saying much to say that we are adaptive problem solvers. We're not rational calculating machines, but biological pattern recognizers who are able to learn from our mistakes. This ignores an awful lot, but this simple starting point, as we saw last chapter, is already enough to explain fundamental features of financial markets that have defeated all the more "sophisticated" theories.

But pattern recognition and adaptation, per se, make no explicit use of *other* social atoms. That we exist among others gives us opportunities we wouldn't have otherwise. By imitating—instinctively, or consciously—we find safety and security, or use others as tools or as providers of clues that help us to make our own decisions. This is not by any means always a good thing. As the philosopher Eric Hoffer once noted, "When people are free to do as they please, they usually imitate each other . . . A society which gives unlimited freedom to the individual, more often than not attains a disconcerting sameness."

But that "sameness" runs according to surprising rules. When we change from one technology to another, or make some socially significant shift in behavior, we do so while following seemingly universal patterns of amplification by way of imitation.

But, an awful lot of what is most important in the social world is still missing from all this—the stronger social interactions associated with trust and distrust, spite and envy, directed hatred and animosity, feelings of devotion and responsibility. We might think of imitation as a "weak" kind of interaction among the social particles, where we use each other as information-bearing clues. But there are other kinds of "stronger" interactions. If the weaker social physics binds us into groups of cell-phone buyers or aficionados of Louis Vuitton fashion, it is a stronger social physics, associated somehow with cooperation and competition, that binds together friends and families and communities. We might think of these as the "strong" interactions of the social world, and as we shall see, they too drive us into collective patterns that no individual ever intended.

Chapter 6

THE COOPERATIVE ATOM

A man ought to be a friend to his friend and repay gift with gift. People should meet smiles with smiles and lies with treachery.

—*THE EDDA*, A THIRTEENTH-CENTURY
COLLECTION OF NORSE EPIC VERSE

AROUND EIGHT A.M. local time, December 26, 2004, an earthquake of magnitude 9.15 struck in the Indian Ocean off the coast of Sumatra. The sudden deformation of the ocean floor caused what happened two hours later, at the Khao Lak Beach in Thailand, where American tourist John Thompson took two photos, just seven seconds apart. The first photo shows an empty bay, where hundreds of locals and tourists had gathered to gape at what seemed to be an incredibly low tide. The second photo shows that bay already filled by an apocalyptic onrushing wave—the deadly Asian tsunami. Thompson snapped more photos over his shoulder as he ran and clambered into the upper floors of a hotel, while behind and beneath him an unstoppable wall of water, reinforced by heavy debris, crushed, shattered, and smashed everything in its path. Similar waves all over Asia ultimately took some 283,000 lives and reminded us all of our frailty in the face of the vast forces of nature.[1]

The only force able to match the devastating power of those terrible waves was the determination and strength of those who survived, and the vast outpouring of sympathy worldwide. Within a few weeks, individuals and nations around the planet had given more than $700 million to relief organizations and local governments. People wrote out large checks to strangers they would never meet, living in places they would never visit. Thompson did what thousands of others fortunate enough to survive also did—he stayed in the area, at his own expense, to help distribute aid donations as they flowed in. After a year's time, individuals, companies, and governments had donated more than $13 billion.

For most of us, there is nothing mysterious about any of this. Among the noblest of human characteristics stands our capacity to sacrifice so that others may be happier or healthier. People dive into raging rivers to save children; some do the same for their pets. After the planes hit the towers of the World Trade Center on September 11, 2001, one man died because he stayed in the building with a paraplegic coworker, while employees in another office carried a disabled colleague and her wheelchair down sixty flights of stairs. In his book *Utmost Savagery*, which tells the terrible story of the titanic U.S.–Japanese battle for the island of Iwo Jima in the Second World War, Colonel Joseph Alexander of the U.S. Marine Corps tells of an American soldier, one hand already blown off, who took a grenade and charged straight into a pillbox, a deliberate act of suicide, in order to save many of his comrades.[2]

Self-sacrifice ranks highly among the moral principles espoused by every culture on earth. Nevertheless, it poses a deep puzzle. Moral high-mindedness and personal self-sacrifice ultimately face up to harsh biological reality. Evolution does not look kindly upon organisms that forgo their own interests to serve the well-being of others. A lioness with cubs would never willingly give her fresh kill, gained at the expense of precious time and energy, to a pack of wild dogs, or even another pride of lions, in the hope they might appreciate the gesture. Grizzlies don't feel compassion for the salmon they slaughter, or anything but aggression toward same-sex grizzlies living nearby. And it's no wonder, given that evolution is all about cutthroat competition. Even plants struggle against each other to reach the light, and microbes wage biochemical warfare.

In fact, the consensus among biologists and social theorists alike is that humans are just as selfish as any other organism; that any apparent selflessness results either from simple blunders, or from selfishness taking on some clever disguise. For example, biologists know how pure self-interest can quite naturally lead to apparent altruism among close genetic relatives. Biologically speaking, our genes have their own "interests," principally to reproduce copies of themselves in coming generations. To improve the chance of success, my genes make me care about my own welfare, as well as that of my children. Less obviously, they also make me care about that of my siblings, half of whose genes are identical to my own, and of my cousins, each of whom has a fourth of my genes. In the eyes of the "selfish gene," helping siblings or cousins survive is just a way of helping our own genes into the future. You may be devoted to a brother or sister and gladly give a kidney to keep him or her alive, but there's nothing necessarily selfless about this, despite appearances.[3]

Economists have argued that other kinds of disguised greed explain why we tip waiters and do favors for colleagues at work, or why, for example, the German race-car driver Michael Schumacher would give a staggering $10 million donation to the tsunami relief effort. That tip today goes in exchange, we hope, for better service next week. Those colleagues will return our favors in the future, quite possibly when we really need a helping hand. And, Michael Schumacher, like any public figure, knows the importance and value of a good public image. Long ago, the seventeenth-century English philosopher Thomas Hobbes summed up the standard economic view of human motivation: "Every man is presumed to seek what is good for himself naturally, and what is just, only for Peace's sake, and accidentally."[4]

But is this really the whole story? Is there really no "true" selflessness in human action? What about all those soldiers through history who have faced extreme danger to save fallen comrades? What about the ordinary people who risked their lives to hide Jews in Nazi-occupied Europe? "Seen through the lens of modern self-interest theory," as economist Robert Frank has noted, "such behavior is the human equivalent of planets moving in square orbits."[5]

In this chapter, I want to look at another aspect of the social atom—our disposition when it comes to interaction with other social atoms. We've seen how the social atom solves problems and makes mistakes, and how it uses other social atoms in its environment as clues, often imitating their behavior and, sometimes, gaining advantages from doing so. But we haven't yet considered how the social atom interacts head to head with others, in competition and cooperation. Of course, everyone is different. But across the globe, from Western cultures to the Far East, from the most advanced societies to the most primitive, people show consistent trends in the way we negotiate human interactions. Research over the past decade appears finally to have put the nail in the coffin of the theory of self-interest. As it turns out, self-interest accounts for only part of our interactions with others, and many of us are not nearly so greedy as economic theorists have long assumed. Moreover, something like true, unspoiled human altruism does really seem to exist, and quite commonly.

What is even more surprising, perhaps, is that the explanation of such behavior appears to require a concerted exploration of the social physics of how individual behavior leads to larger collective patterns when many social atoms get together. As we shall see, our "prosocial" disposition and our noblest altruistic tendencies have deep roots in the physics of social self-organization and are probably responsible for our species' unparalleled success in coordinating large groups and institutions—everything from corner shops to multinational corporations, from communities to large governments.

BEING A NICE GUY... SELFISHLY

The standard explanation of human cooperation rests entirely on the idea that we do things for others only because we hope to get something for ourselves. It is no surprise, of course, that two people cooperate when they both benefit immediately from doing so. If one farmer has two ploughs and a horse, and another has two horses and a plough, they can exchange horse for plough temporarily and both gain, without risk. But a lot of human cooperation requires the negotiation of tricky situations in which both parties stand to gain, yet also face a strong risk of being cheated. Even 250 years ago, the Scottish philosopher and historian David Hume put his finger on the nub of the dilemma:

> Your corn is ripe today; mine will be so tomorrow. 'Tis profitable for us both, that I shou'd labour with you to-day, and that you shou'd aid me to-morrow. I have no kindness for you,

and know you have as little for me. I will not, therefore, take any pains on your account; and should I labour with you upon my own account, in expectation of a return, I know I shou'd be disappointed, and that I shou'd in vain depend upon your gratitude. Here then I leave you to labour alone: You treat me in the same manner. The seasons change; and both of us lose our harvests for want of mutual confidence and security.[6]

This disastrous outcome is no surprise according to modern game theory, a mainstay of mathematical economics, which predicts that self-interested beings should always fail to cooperate under such circumstances. Essentially restating Hume's argument, the theory reasons as follows: If two strictly self-interested farmers face the harvest dilemma only once, the best outcome for either is to get his neighbor to help with his own harvest, without ever having to make a similar effort of his own. Knowing this, neither farmer will be willing to stick his neck out, laboring for his neighbor on the first day, as he knows he'll surely be cheated on the second day. So two farmers—if they meet only once, an important point as we shall see—will refuse to cooperate.[7]

But of course people do routinely cooperate in these kinds of situations. How they manage it, as social theorists well understand, is often by way of a mechanism for establishing and maintaining trust that biologists refer to as reciprocal altruism. In essence, everything changes if two people meet repeatedly. In the case of the farmers, they may face such harvest situations every year, as well as many similar farming problems in between times when mutual aid can be beneficial to both. In this case, treachery on the part of one farmer, in any encounter, comes at a high cost—the breakdown of trust and probable retaliation by the other farmer through his refusal to cooperate. Repetition changes the logic entirely, as it allows a kind of "discussion" to take place between the two parties. Each will continue to cooperate as long as the other does. Any attempt to cheat will promptly be punished by refusal to cooperate at the next opportunity. As political scientist Robert Axelrod of the University of Michigan demonstrated in his classic work *The Evolution of Cooperation*, the logic applies not only to farmers, but to anyone facing similar scenarios in which cooperation can pay, but cheating is a threat.[8]

In 1915, Captain Geoffrey Dugdale of the British army arrived with fresh soldiers at the English–German lines in Belgium. He and his men were to replace exhausted troops in the trenches. But in the few days before getting into the line, Dugdale was astonished by what he saw—British soldiers apparently taking it easy on the enemy, showing no inclination to shoot even at clear targets. There were, Dugdale later recalled, "German soldiers walking about within rifle range behind their own line. Our men appeared to take no notice. I privately made up my mind to do away with that sort of thing when we took over; such things should not be allowed. These people evidently did not know there was a war on. Both sides apparently believed in the policy of 'live and let live.' "[9]

Such behavior may have been puzzling to Dugdale, but it is not puzzling from a logical point of view. After an initial bloody phase of the war in which troops were relatively mobile, the First World War settled into stagnant trench warfare with units facing one another across a wasteland of a few hundred yards. The same men faced each other for many months at a time. Both sides had everything to lose by prolonged heavy bombardments, and everything to gain if they could somehow agree to take it easy on one another. The two sides learned to cooperate, through repeated interaction, meeting the enemy's cooperation with their own, and punishing any transgression with extreme violence. Ex-soldiers recalled artillery being fired to a consistent schedule and with predictable placement, each side showing their skills to the enemy—as an implicit warning—while also showing their willingness to avoid enemy casualties. As one soldier put it, "The real reason for the quietness of some sections of the line was that neither side had any intention of advancing in that particular district . . . If the British shelled the Germans, the Germans replied, and the damage was equal: if the Germans bombed an advanced piece of trench and killed five Englishmen, an answering fusillade killed five Germans."[10]

Troops upon leaving the front would teach their replacements about the desirability of the effective agreement. "Mr. Bosche ain't a bad fellow. You leave 'im alone; 'e'll leave you alone."[11]

In ultimate terms, of course, reciprocal altruism of this kind isn't really altruism at all, just a clever strategy for getting the most for oneself out of a tricky situation. Over the past thirty or forty years, many biologists and social theorists have come to believe that similar strategic thinking lies behind all altruism, and that altruists always aim to get something in return for their kindness; it is always selfishness in disguise. Reciprocal altruism is only one of several mechanisms that researchers have identified by which the self-interested can give something now to get something later. Through acts of kindness a person can build up a useful reserve of goodwill or obligation in others. Selfless acts help a person build a reputation as someone to be trusted, something that person can cash in on later.

In any situation in which cheating is possible, "strategic" cooperation of this kind among self-interested parties requires repeated interactions, so that one person can use his or her own cooperation as strategic bait to coax cooperation out of others.

Take away any opportunity for repetition, for encounters in the future, and cooperation should wither like a flower in a waterless desert. The heartening story of "live and let live" from the First World War, carried a little further, offers a depressing illustration. Toward the end of the war, when tanks were introduced and the battle became more fluid and troops more mobile, troops no longer faced one another in repeated encounters over extended periods. Instances of the "live and let live" logic disappeared as well.

The preceding offers an extremely brief summary of mainstream thinking on the puzzle of human cooperation—until fairly recently. Much of it still stands as good wisdom, as the social atom is in many cases selfish and cooperates out of strategic motives. There is little doubt that we are inherently good game players; studies have even shown that we seem to have devoted biological mechanisms for detecting cheaters. For example, we are generally better at perceiving subtle patterns when the setting involves cues concerning possibilities of cheating than when it does not. Take the following puzzle. Suppose you've recently moved to the Boston suburbs, and someone tells you that anyone traveling into the center of Boston will take the subway. Now look at the following four cards:

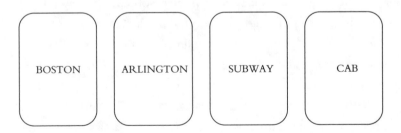

One side of each card gives the place a certain person went to, and the other side shows how they traveled. Now your task: indicate *only* those cards that you need to turn over to see if any of this information violates what you were told about people going to Boston always taking the subway.

From a logical point of view, the answer is the first and last card. You need to check the first card, because this person went to Boston, and so the other side had better say "Subway." You also need to check the last card, as this person traveled by cab, and so the other side of the card had better not say "Boston." If you struggled to get the right answer, don't worry too much—in most experiments with this kind of thing, only about 25 percent of people get the right answer. But now for the interesting part. Let's do the test over, leaving the logic of the situation entirely unchanged, but altering the content of the information. Now suppose you are told that the children in some school are allowed cookies in the afternoon, but only if they've helped clean the playroom. Each card will now give information, for a certain child, about whether they helped clean, on one side, and about whether they ate cookies on the other. So now we have:

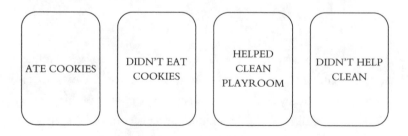

Again, you have to point out only those cards you need to turn over to make sure that no child is violating the rule. Again, the answer is the first and last cards. Did this seem easier? In experiments of this kind, about 65 percent of people tend to get the right answer, which somehow just seems to "pop out" from the page, apparently because the content somehow excites our minds to process the material differently. It's obvious that you don't need to check anyone who hasn't eaten cookies, or who has helped clean, as these people couldn't possibly violate the rule. Only those who have eaten cookies or who didn't help clean need to be checked. A variety of experiments along these lines suggest that we have deep instincts for detecting cheating, presumably because learning to cooperate with others, while not being cheated, was of such vital importance in our evolutionary past.[12]

But if we are clearly skilled at detecting cheaters, this alone does not imply that we are only willing to cooperate in the context of ongoing relationships. If social theorists have learned one thing in the past two decades, it is that real people do not always act as tidy theories say they should. The logic of pure self-interest implies that all altruism should completely disappear if people have no hope whatsoever of gaining anything in the future. But as it now appears, this is simply not true—some of us seem to be "true altruists" after all.

OUR SOCIAL INSTINCTS

Suppose I bring you into a room, sit you next to a complete stranger, and give you $100. I then say that you have to offer some of the money to the stranger, however much you like, from $1 up to the full $100. If the stranger accepts your offer, then you both get to keep the amounts in question. But if the stranger rejects the offer, you have to give the entire $100 back to me. You are only going to do this one time, and then you and the stranger will go your separate ways and you'll never see one another again. What would you do?

If you're a true rationalist, and if you're convinced that all human behavior is ultimately based on the rational pursuit of self-interest, the choice is dead easy. You are only meeting once, and the stranger, being self-interested, doesn't have much of a choice. Whatever you offer, he or she can either take it or leave it. As getting some money is obviously better than getting no money, the stranger will take it. So you can offer as little as you like—say, $1—in full confidence that it'll be accepted. You'll come away with $99.

The logic of economic game theory is so definitive on this point that this gamelike situation—known technically as the Ultimatum Game—doesn't warrant even passing interest from theorists. It's a no-brainer, which probably explains why no one even got around to testing this game with real people until about fifteen years ago. Why do experiments if the outcomes are foregone conclusions? The answer, of course, is that science knows nothing more dangerous than trusting in the inherent beauty and consistency of pure logic. Fortunately, researchers over the past decade or so have come to recognize that the best way to discover the rules of human behavior isn't to dwell on the theoretical advantages of perfect rationality or pure greed, but to treat the social atom the way physicists treat real atoms—by doing experiments in the laboratory to probe and prod their thoughts and emotions. The Ultimatum Game offers a prime example.

By now researchers have run literally hundreds of studies of this game, typically with student volunteers. The usual approach is to have students play in random pairs with about $10 or $20 at stake. To theorists' consternation, what these "one-shot"

experiments consistently show is that most people, when "pro-
posers," offer about 40 percent of the money, either because they
feel this is fair or because they worry that a smaller offer will be
rejected. Meanwhile, about half of all "receivers" reject offers at
the 20 percent level, even if the stakes rise up to several hundred
dollars. Clearly, few of the students behave in accordance with
the postulates of self-interest.

These results run so counter to economists' expectations that
many, at first, simply refused to accept them. For example, some
theorists objected that the players could see one another during
the game, could learn each other's face, and so might anticipate
running into one another later. This might account for their cooperative behavior, through the ordinary logic of reciprocal altruism.
But researchers have now run the experiment many times with
players operating with complete anonymity through computers, so
there can be no chance of future considerations having any effect.
The results always remain the same—people still cooperate. Another objection of traditional self-interest theorists is that since
most of the volunteers have been students, the results might only
say something about the unrepresentative behavior of hopelessly
naïve and idealistic students. But further experiments have demol-
ished even this desperate attempt to salvage orthodoxy.

Two years ago, a team led by anthropologist Joseph Henrich of
Emory University carried out anonymous, one-shot Ultimatum
Game experiments with individuals from fifteen different cultures scattered around the globe, from the Sango farmers of Tan-
zania to the Machiguenga in Peru. To make their participants
take the game seriously, they set the stakes at one day's or two
days' wages in these cultures. They found that people in some
cultures were incredibly generous. Among the Aché of northeast-
ern Paraguay and the Lamelara of Indonesia, for example, the

mean offers were actually above 50 percent of the stake. More important, however, all cultures were alike in deviating systematically from the economic "ideal" of strict self-interest, even the stingiest offering at least 25 percent of the stake on average. Across the board, the "receivers" in the experiments typically rejected offers of less than about 25 percent. As Henrich and his colleagues concluded, "In addition to their own material payoffs, many experimental subjects appear to care about fairness and reciprocity, are willing to change the distribution of material outcomes at personal cost, and are willing to reward those who act in a cooperative manner while punishing those who do not even when these actions are costly to the individual."[13]

To be sure there's nothing peculiar about the Ultimatum Game, researchers have also run lots of other experiments, different in their technical details, but all designed to elicit the same essential dilemma for those involved—a stark choice between pursuing their own self-interest for easy gain, or instead, and at a cost to themselves, conforming to social norms of fairness. To take one example, a minor variant of the Ultimatum Game is the Dictator Game. This is exactly the same except that the "receiver" now has no option to refuse what is offered. The proposer—the Dictator—simply decides how much to give and that's it. Even here, without any threat of rejection, many people still offer a reasonable fraction of the pie to the other person, apparently out of a sense of fairness.[14] Across the board, experiments like this show that people of all kinds tend to be what economists now call strong reciprocators—people who will stick their necks out to be reciprocal in their relations with others, to cooperate without any hope of future gains, or to punish those who they feel are not cooperating.

Somewhat disturbingly, it is curious to note that research also suggests that the culture of modern economic theory may have an insidious influence on how economists themselves behave in comparison to "normal" people. One study, for example, looked at how graduate students from different disciplines played the co-operative games akin to the situation of the farmers described by David Hume.[15] Students from psychology and mathematics played it much as other people do. The one group that stood out were graduate students of economics, who had apparently absorbed the conviction that others will always act on their self-interest and so acted that way themselves—they refused to cooperate far more frequently than other students. In effect, studying economics—at least economics as it has been taught in the past—seems to make people greedy. As the authors of the study put it, "Exposure to the self-interest model does in fact encourage self-interested behavior." This is a somewhat worrying observation, I think, given the vast influence that economists have as advisers to many of the world's governments.

In conclusion, the altruism observed in these experiments does really seem to be something like "true" altruism, something that makes absolutely no sense from the point of view of the theory of self-interest. With this new picture of the social atom—based on evidence rather than conjecture—it now seems that all those donations to the victims of the tsunami weren't really so unusual after all, but represent a common pattern among people. And yet observing a pattern in human behavior is not the same thing as explaining it. We still face the troubling fact that any organism that helps others at its own expense stands at an important evolutionary disadvantage. How can such altruism be explained, scientifically?

THE ROOTS OF KINDNESS

Superficially, it might seem as if our emotions explain everything in one stroke. Put bluntly, acting altruistically makes us feel good. We feel like good people when we help others, and a little guilty when we're stingy. We get an emotional payoff in repaying our obligations to others, or in getting even with someone who has wronged us. To weigh up the pros and cons of any action, an individual has to count not only external payoffs, but internal as well. Most people feel this to be true from their own experience. Modern brain imaging during economic experiments backs it up. Several years before his experiments on social conformity, Gregory Burns led a team of researchers who had volunteers face one another in a situation like the farmers' dilemma, where both could gain by cooperating but each also had an incentive to cheat, getting even more at the other's expense. The imaging monitor showed that when the players cooperated, the most active parts of their brains included the nucleus accumbens and the orbitofrontal cortex—areas associated with processing emotional rewards.[16] In 2004, economist Ernst Fehr and psychologist Dominique de Quervain of the University of Zürich discovered in similar experiments that we get a mental buzz when we punish cheaters, even when it means incurring a personal monetary cost.[17]

But all of this is really only a partial or "proximate" explanation. Organisms can't live off their emotional payoffs; they need food, shelter, and mates. The deeper issue is why we have such emotions at all, and how they help us biologically, especially emotions that drive people to "extreme" acts of altruism, such as soldiers falling on grenades to save their comrades. Is there any conceivable way such acts could make biological sense? And if not, why hasn't evolution wiped out of existence people who have such emotions and act on them? This puzzle is a matter of ongoing scientific controversy.

One possibility is that evolution is actually wiping such people out, but just hasn't yet finished the job. It is important to recall again that we humans have not always lived as we do today. As the authors of a NASA report in the 1960s noted, the conditions of the familiar modern world have existed for only a tiny slice of our human existence:

> Eight hundred life spans can bridge more than 50,000 years. But of these 800 people, 650 spent their lives in caves or worse; only the last 70 had any truly effective means of communicating with one another, only the last 6 ever saw a printed word or had any real means of measuring heat or cold, only the last 4 could measure time with any precision; only the last 2 used an electric motor; and the vast majority of the items that make up our material world were developed within the life span of the 800th person.[18]

To gain any deep understanding of our current behavior, we need to recognize that our ancestors throughout virtually all of human history lived in small, isolated groups of hunter-gatherers. Anthropologists refer to this period as the Environment of Evolutionary Adaptiveness—the environment in which our ancestors lived for 99 percent of human history. During this time, what would have happened daily, throughout countless human lives over thousands of generations, was repeated interactions among the members of these small groups. In other words, it is a certainty that our ancestors were steeped, through unending real-world experience, in the logic of reciprocal altruism. We are here today in large part because our ancestors absorbed this logic into the fabric of their minds and, because of it, drew the benefits of cooperation.

Obviously, a deeply ingrained biological affinity for reciprocal altruism cannot directly explain the true altruism found in modern experiments, where anonymous players meet only once. Reciprocal altruism, as a sensible strategy, requires repetition. But many evolutionary biologists and anthropologists think that our habits may be so deeply ingrained that they lead us into instinctive errors. Take someone into the laboratory, explain carefully that they are playing a game only once and with someone whom they will never see again, and the message may not really sink in. It may reach the conscious level, perhaps, but not deeply enough to influence their behavior. Like those university students who made instinctive errors in simple arithmetic problems, people in these experiments might just make mistakes when facing one-shot situations, treating them *as if* they were actually in a repeated interaction. The authors of a well-argued recent paper asserting this position put it as follows: "Our brains were shaped in a world that conferred net gains to those who granted initial generous outlays and punished cheats. This bias toward cooperation stems from a brain design selected over millions of years. Not surprisingly, therefore, it has persisted into the latest fraction of a percent of our history in which we find ourselves in cities, civilization and anonymous, one-shot laboratory experiments with strangers."[19]

If this idea is right, then strong reciprocity is only a "maladaptation." We learned through 99 percent of our evolutionary history that interactions with other social atoms were always repeat interactions, and now we find it hard to act differently when put into an artificial laboratory setting carefully construed to produce one-shot interactions. In such artificial situations, we're tricked into doing things that are most definitely not in our self-interest. This would make strong reciprocity just another in a long list of modern maladaptations found in modern human behavior, like some of the inbuilt thinking errors we explored in chapter 3. It would be no more surprising than the stimulation of sexual excitement by a film or photograph, even though such desire originally evolved to further procreation.

This idea seems plausible. But there are plenty of arguments against it too. For example, it is by no means clear that our ancestors only ever had interactions with others in their own small group. Especially during crises, after a rare flood or during a drought, for example, individuals from such groups would have ventured far and wide in search of water holes or animal herds and would almost certainly have encountered strangers from other groups. Far from their normal territory, they'd have little chance of ever meeting again. Using data on the travels of modern hunter-gatherers, Henrich estimates that critical one-shot situations of this kind would have happened fairly frequently:

> If one were to "reverse engineer" from the available empirical evidence back to the ancestral environment (the EEA—Environment of Evolutionary Adaptiveness) that characterized human evolution, one would predict that our ancestors had frequent encounters with strangers, and that these encounters had substantial fitness consequences . . . data from small-scale foraging societies and chimpanzees clearly shows that interactions with strangers were likely common and highly fitness relevant.[20]

Moreover, such encounters were likely to be dangerous given the stakes—with each person representing his tribe in the midst of a life-and-death crisis. Evolution would not be kind to those who tended to treat such one-shot encounters as if they were repeated interactions, offering a hand in a spirit of cooperation only to be hacked to death. Maladaptation of this kind should, it would seem, have been stamped out long ago.

If so, then strong reciprocity remains a puzzle. But another possible explanation is, perhaps, more natural—that strong reciprocity might fundamentally be involved with the basic physics of social cohesion, and a key element of the social mechanics that enabled our ancestors to form functioning, cohesive groups. It may indeed lie at the heart of what makes us the most social of all animals.

THE PHYSICS OF SOCIAL COHESION

No one likes paying taxes. Even so, we need taxes if we want roads with functioning traffic lights, an educated public, programs to ensure public health through vaccines, and an army to defend us. These are what economists call public goods—things from which everyone benefits whether he or she personally helps pay for them or not—and as social theorists well understand, this disconnect between paying and enjoying can lead to big social trouble. After all, if everyone can enjoy the good whether he or she contributes or not, then everyone has a temptation to cheat—to use the roads, for example, but to let others pay for them. The ultimate outcome is social dysfunction—the famous "tragedy of the commons."

In 1968 an economist named Gareth Hardin first drew the clear outlines of this problem, one of the most fundamental in all social science.[21] Hardin used a simple parable. Imagine a village with a central pasture of rich grassland where everyone can graze his or her cattle. The pasture is a public good that benefits the community as a whole. So that the grass can replenish itself, the villagers need to limit the total amount of grazing. Unfortunately, if the village has no system in place to restrict grazing and counts on the people to manage it themselves, it will succumb to a group version of the farmers' failure that David Hume envisioned so long ago. If everyone is strictly self-interested, then it's in no one's individual interest to limit the grazing of his or her own cattle, suspecting that his or her neighbors won't limit theirs. Knowing that the mob might just destroy the pasture tomorrow, I'll take my cattle to graze today—and so will you. The inevitable result—everyone tries to get his or her share before it's gone, overgrazing destroys the commons, to everyone's detriment, all from a failure of the underlying social physics to provide a mechanism for sustainable cooperation.

Like other social phenomena, the tragedy of the commons can quite easily be demonstrated in the laboratory. For example, Ernst Fehr and colleagues at the University of Zürich have studied volunteers playing a "public goods" game. In this game, each of a handful of players starts out with some money, say $10, and, in each round, has to choose how much to contribute to a "public fund." Each can give anything from $0 up to $10. Once they make their contributions, the experimenter collects the funds, doubles their value, and distributes the result equally back to the players. The doubling is crucial, as it is meant to reflect that investments in public goods—in roads, fields, or whatever—give the overall group a positive return. The more everyone contributes, the more they each get back. If everyone contributes $10, then with $40 in the pot, the experimenter would give back a total of $2 \times \$40 = \$80$ among the players, or $20 to each. Each makes a healthy profit of $10.

What makes the game interesting, however, is that people have an incentive to cheat. If everyone else contributes, a player does even better by cheating and contributing nothing. For example, if one person gives nothing, while the others give $10, then the experimenter distributes 2×$30=$60, giving $15 to each. The nongiver makes $15 in addition to his kept $10. In the experiments, the temptation to take this extra profit spoils the cooperative show. Researchers find that in early rounds of the game, a strong spirit of cooperation prevails. Although truly self-interested people would always cheat, most players, being strong reciprocators, start out contributing generously, and the group as a whole profits. But a small fraction of people do cheat, and their behavior soon has an insidious effect on the rest. Other players begin to notice the cheating, and no one wants to be a sucker, subsidizing the cheaters' profits. With each round, players became increasingly distrustful of others and retaliate by cheating themselves. After ten rounds, public spiritedness had decayed to the point where most players contribute nothing.[22]

This simple experiment suggests that narrow-minded self-interest is not sufficient to support the emergence of sustained cooperation within large groups. Theoretical studies have come to much the same conclusion: that reciprocal altruism and other ways to establish cooperation among self-interested actors seem to work only in groups of a handful of people. When numbers get to, say, thirty or fifty, forget it. Until recently, social theorists only knew of one solution to this dilemma—you guessed it, government, or at least a powerful someone or something with a big stick who can force people to contribute to their collective welfare and to refrain from cheating through a credible threat of punishment. It is because of government that we (or most of us, anyway) pay our taxes.

But by experimenting further with social atoms in the laboratory, putting them together under different conditions to see what might happen, researchers have now discovered another way to avoid the tragedy of the commons—a recipe for cooperation that may be one of the deepest secrets of human social organization. In a variation of their original experiments, Fehr and his colleagues made it possible for any individual, at a cost to themselves of $1, to fine a player who they felt had not contributed enough in the preceding round. It would cost the finer $1, while the person fined would lose $2, given over to the public fund. People who levy fines obviously get nothing directly in return; they just lose $1. Yet spurred by a sense of outrage at those they saw cheating, many volunteers in the experiments were quite willing to do this, despite the cost. With the threat of punishment in place, cheating became less tempting, and the history of the experiment changed—after ten rounds, cooperation persisted. With strong reciprocity, it seems, stable cooperation can emerge and persist all on its own.[23]

The outcome of these simple experiments begins to look potentially profound when we look back at our hunter-gatherer ancestors. There were no governments in those days, yet these groups depended utterly on unfailing cooperation for their existence—to gather food, to hunt big animals, and to defend themselves against other groups. As it now appears, strong reciprocity may be just the behavioral characteristic, the social glue, that helped those social atoms to achieve it—in effect, the "physics" at the individual level that gives rise naturally to cooperation and cohesion at the collective level, much as attraction among atoms can lead to a cohesive solid. We may be strong reciprocators today because it is what helped our ancestors form cohesive groups that won out in the harsh struggle for existence, while our more self-interested cousins in the distant past failed to cooperate and died out as a result.

Mathematical support for this idea comes from the theoretical studies of economist Herbert Gintis of the University of Massachusetts Amherst, anthropologist Robert Boyd of the University of California at Los Angeles, and others. They've run extensive computer simulations to explore the natural competition that would have prevailed both within and between early groups of hunter-gatherers. Such groups would constantly have been competing with each other for territory, food, and mates, and the ability to forge effective large-scale cooperation would obviously have been profoundly advantageous. Crucially, they included two effects in their simulations. First, within any group, the individuals are competing for food, mates, and so on. Here strong reciprocity is no advantage; in fact, it is a clear disadvantage as such people would be exploited by more selfish members of the group. By the ordinary workings of evolution, you should therefore expect the number of strong reciprocators to slowly dwindle. If this were the only force at work, they would have disappeared long ago.

But another process works in precisely the opposite direction— the competition of groups amongst themselves, with those who are more cooperative generally doing better. It is natural to expect that groups with a higher fraction of strong reciprocators will tend to win battles against groups with fewer or would have a better chance of surviving a long drought through their effective collective action. So group-level competition should tend to cull groups of the self-interested and preserve those with many altruists. Gintis and Boyd have shown that if this group-level competition is strong enough—as it plausibly was in those times—it would have been enough to keep a high fraction of strong reciprocators around in the general human population. In effect, being an altruist doesn't help you personally, but it does help the group of which you are a part. The more cooperation becomes important to group survival, the more you should expect true altruism to exist—because it helped our ancestors' groups survive through the cruelest circumstances. (To spell out the logic bluntly, selection acting between individuals should work against strong reciprocity, but selection between groups should work for it. If competition between groups is important enough, then strong reciprocity should naturally evolve.)

These findings suggest that true altruism, far from being a maladaptation, may in fact be the key to our species' success by providing the social glue that allowed our ancestors to form strong, resilient groups. We're not so greedy and self-centered after all. Something like real kindness probably had to evolve, and it is probably still crucial for a lot of social cohesion that makes today's world better than it would be. We are biologically steeped in the habits of cooperation.

OUR STRANGELY "COLLECTIVE" SELVES

In July of 1793, a young woman in her midtwenties named Charlotte Corday traveled secretly from Caen on the west coast of France to Paris. The following day, with a long knife purchased in the marketplace, she went to the home of Jean-Paul Marat, a ruthless figure in the French Revolution, and stabbed him to death. Corday did not attempt to flee from the police, but turned herself in peacefully, sacrificing her life, intentionally, for what she felt was the good of her country. On the day of her execution, one week later, she wrote a letter to her father:

> Forgive me, my dear Papa, for having disposed of my existence without your permission. I have avenged many innocent victims and I have prevented many other disasters. The people one day, undeceived, will rejoice to have been delivered from a

tyrant . . . I beg you to forgive me, or, rather, to rejoice at my fate. The cause of it is glorious.[24]

To really explain why Charlotte Corday gave her life for the benefit of her people would of course require a detailed history of her upbringing and personality, her experiences before and during the French Revolution, of what she had heard about this Mr. Marat and his role in events, and why she felt that his death would make things better. An explanation of the selfless acts of the New York City firefighters on 9/11 would likewise have to delve into their personalities, and the life experiences that had led them to become firefighters—to put themselves in a position widely acknowledged to involve the risk of death. The same holds true for any full explanation of a truly selfless act by any person, anywhere at any time.

But explaining why biology would ever permit anyone to perform truly altruistic acts, steeped as it is in the harsh calculus of survival, is a question for science, not history or psychology. The traditional view of the social atom as unfailingly greedy and self-interested is simply false. It fails to account at all for selfless actions that millions of people undertake every day without any strategic hope of future rewards. Many of us appear to be biologically predisposed to such altruistic acts. We may not give our lives, but we lend a hand or give money and time to help others, without any greedy overtones or expectations about what is coming back to us in the future. People give directions to perfect strangers on street corners, find lost letters and take time to post them again, return purses containing money.

The postulates of self-interest cannot account for the large-scale cooperation we find routinely in communities, businesses, universities, and clubs everywhere. And we are beginning to see why—it appears that selfless behavior may exist precisely because it is a key characteristic of the social atom that makes such large-scale cooperation readily possible. Throughout the ages, groups endowed with such altruists have outperformed those without them, leading naturally to such behavior being spread more widely. As we have seen earlier in this book, understanding this point seems to require a perspective of simplicity rather than complexity. It means getting a good basic picture of the social atom, putting lots of such atoms together, and then seeing what surprises emerge. In this case, we see that the way we are as individuals depends not so much on how our behavior helps us, as individuals, but on how it influences the collective behavior of the groups we are part of. Our habits cannot easily be separated from the behavior of the groups to which we belong. And if it is true, as Robert Wright argues in his book *Nonzero*, that human history can be best understood as the long struggle between groups of greater or less cooperative skills, with the more skilled tending to win out, then we should not be surprised that we, the descendants of the winners, are virtually hardwired for cooperation.[25]

Much as the forces of electricity and magnetism lead to the laws of chemistry, we see that the peculiarly altruistic character of the social atom leads to ready cooperation in our societies. Economists have long been puzzled as to why many companies pay their employees more than they absolutely have to, given what those employees would get elsewhere. They've similarly been puzzled as to why many employees will work with an energy and devotion to the company that far exceeds what they are paid. These and many other apparent "anomalies" of ordinary life now appear as anomalies only if one refuses to accept a more realistic picture of the social atom as one that cares about the groups he or she is part of and works with a sense of fairness that goes far beyond purely monetary considerations.[26]

But the strongly reciprocal character of the social atom isn't all good. As we shall see in the next chapter, it also has a dark side. One of the key elements of the apparent evolutionary origins of strong reciprocity is a deep connection with one's own group— a willingness to cooperate with them even without any hope of individual gain. The flip side of this coin is a deeply ingrained tendency in many of us to fear and distrust, perhaps even despise, those from other groups. We were all surprised and shocked when, in what was then Yugoslavia, the uncivilized savagery of the Middle Ages erupted into the heart of modern Europe. A better picture of the social atom suggests that we shouldn't have been surprised, because the group hatred and suspicion that drives ethnic conflict may go hand in hand with our nobler gifts for charity. The deepest paradox of social physics may be this— we are inherently skilled at making peace for the same reasons that we are skilled at making war.

Chapter 7

TOGETHER, APART

The great power of science is its ability, through brutal objectivity, to reveal to us truth we did not anticipate.
—ROBERT LAUGHLIN

B Y JULY OF 1995, journalist Samantha Power of the *Washington Post* had covered the brutal conflict between Bosnian Muslims and Serbs for nearly two years. She had interviewed the traumatized survivors of concentration camps and mass rapes, and those who had seen their families executed before their eyes. She had witnessed hatred of maniacal intensity fueled by a fantastic lust to avenge historic battles lost six or seven centuries before. But it is not easy for a mind accustomed to the dependable normality of human civilization to comprehend fully the realm of possibilities beyond it. As Power later recalled, memories of her personal experiences, even then, seemed strangely blunted, almost "imaginary":

I had worked in Sarajevo, where Serb snipers took target practice on bundled old ladies hauling canisters of filthy water across town and where picturesque parks had been transformed into cemeteries to accommodate the deluge of young arrivals. I had interviewed emaciated men who had dropped 40 or 50 pounds and bore permanent scars from their time in Serb concentration camps. And I had only recently covered the massacre of four schoolgirls. Yet despite my experiences, or perhaps because of them, I could only imagine what I had already witnessed.

Being thus distanced from the reality about her, it was with no great alarm, in Srebrenica on July 11, that Power heard the news that Serb forces under General Ratko Mladic had just taken the city. They had done so despite its being proclaimed a "safe area" by the United Nations. Like others, Power assumed that the Bosnian Serbs would do nothing that might provoke a forceful international military response. She was strangely unprepared for what happened next: "A few days after Srebrenica fell, a colleague of mine telephoned from New York and said the Bosnian Ambassador to the U.N. was claiming that the Bosnian Serbs had murdered more than 1,000 Muslim men from Srebrenica in a football stadium. It was not possible. 'No,' I said simply. My friend repeated the charge. 'No,' I said again, determined."

As it turned out, Power was right—but not in the way she thought. Mladic had not executed one thousand men, but more than seven thousand, all men and boys, in the greatest single slaughter in Europe since the Second World War.[1]

Like Samantha Power, most of us find it difficult, as she put it, "to muster the imagination needed to reckon with evil." We expect, and our experience confirms, that people, but for a few sociopaths, professional criminals, and the like, generally act more or less reasonably and in accordance with peaceful norms. Sane people, ordinary human beings, do not slaughter babies or old women for sport, collect heads and ears as trophies, or force mothers to shoot their own sons. Monstrous things must, we suppose, have monstrous causes. In genocides and comparable eruptions of mass violence we see madness and evil, and our first inclination is to trace such horrors to the twisted character of some people ("those bloodthirsty Serbs") or to some madman or group of madmen, to the likes of Slobodan Milosevic or Ratko Mladic. Either explanation restores a comforting belief that mass killing is not among the "normal" workings of the human world, but the social equivalent of a freak earthquake or volcanic eruption.

But if we accept desirable social outcomes as the natural products of human nature, it seems wrong to reject the undesirable as perverse distortions of it. Viewed empirically, as a part of history, our human capacity for hatred and violence is certainly as natural as our capacity for friendship and cooperation. An authentic explanation of what happened in Bosnia, or at least of how such events can come to pass, should go far beyond talk of madness and evil. After all, the tragedy in Bosnia was hardly unique in human history. Many such disasters—in Rwanda in 1994, or in Armenia in 1915, or in Nazi Germany—were brought about by the energies of millions of ordinary people, most of whom, afterward, went back to ordinary lives. As the Austrian economist Friedrich von Hayek noted during the Second World War, "The supreme tragedy is still not seen that in Germany it was largely people of goodwill, men who were admired and held up as models in the country, who prepared the way, if they did not actually create, the forces which now stand for everything they detest."[2]

In this chapter, I want to explore the outlines of a natural explanation of ethnic hatred and genocide, while building on our simple picture of the social atom. As we saw last chapter, the easy altruism of many people—the tendency toward what we've called strong reciprocity—seems to play an important role in helping us to cooperate and achieve things together. Our ancestors' cooperative skills let them manage the difficult harvests, defend themselves against enemies, or—one must also suspect—make war against and slaughter neighboring groups for their land or resources. In this respect, our altruistic nature, as individuals, has a paradoxical group origin. It cannot be explained as a behavior that helps individuals, as individuals; rather, it only seems to make sense as an aid to social cohesion and has arisen out of a tumultuous history of competition between groups. The implication is that individual human nature itself bears the marks of our collective history.

But there is more to cooperation and group associations than strong reciprocity, or the even more basic you-help-me-I'll-help-you logic of reciprocal altruism. The single most obvious fact about any group is that something has to define it; the members of a group share something, whether it is nationality, skin color, style of clothing, age, the place they live, speaking accent, or even opposition to some other group. Those within the group have the characteristic, and those on the outside do not. It may be unfortunate, but these labels carry psychological force, as many people discriminate on their basis, judging others by their skin color, religion, or style of dress. We rarely ask why we are so skilled at or prone to such discrimination, or why so many of us can, at the drop of a hat, hate others we have never met and know nothing about. As we shall see, the answer is by no means obvious and probably cannot be found just by observing people carefully or scrutinizing the history of racism and nationalism. But social physics does have some things to say about the matter.

At the root of violent nationalistic, racial, or cultural hatred lies a social paradox: the very forces that work to pull us apart are also those that help to keep us together. Incredibly, as we shall see, even blind prejudice may help us to cooperate.

GROUP AFFLICTIONS

In the summer of 1954, social psychologist Muzafer Sherif and colleagues at the University of Oklahoma took twenty-two ordinary boys, all around twelve years old, to a two-hundred-acre Boy Scout camp within the Robbers Cave State Park in Oklahoma. The researchers divided the boys into two groups of eleven, taking care to balance their physical, mental, and social talents. The experiment was designed to explore two things—first, if just putting people into a group and giving them common goals would be enough to make a hierarchy emerge, with individuals taking on distinct roles, and second, if competition between groups would trigger strong group identification and loyalty, despite the completely arbitrary nature of how the groups were put together.

At first, the scientists kept the two groups apart. After a few days of "team building" exercises, some boys had become leaders and others followers, and each group had invented a group name; henceforth, they were the Eagles and the Rattlers. A few more days and both groups were boasting of their own remarkable prowess and mocking the sad lot of misfits in the other group— none of whom they had, at this point, actually met. Things got a little more hostile when the researchers announced that there would be a competition. The Rattlers occupied the baseball diamond, fixing their flag to the backstop, and threatened to beat up any Eagle foolish enough to use the field for practice. When the two groups finally met face-to-face, they hurled insults and sang derisive songs, like ancient enemies. The animosity escalated over the next few days, as each group tried to burn the other's flag.

Sherif and his colleagues' study has the elegant simplicity of a physics experiment.[3] Put some atoms over here in one group, and some others over there in another. Let the two groups interact and watch what happens. When the atoms are people—or at least twelve-year-old American boys—you get two things: a strong attachment of the atoms to their own group, and animosity toward outsiders. Of course, "in group" prejudice of this kind affects a lot more than twelve-year-old boys.

The few remaining tribes on earth who live in isolation and in conditions like all of mankind one hundred thousand years ago still cultivate an extreme intolerance of anyone outside their group. On January 27, 2005, two unfortunate Indian fishermen, apparently drunk on palm wine, drifted onto the beach of North Sentinel Island, part of the Andaman Islands in the Bay of Bengal. They were promptly set upon and hacked to death by loin-clothed warriors of the Sentinelese, who inhabit the island. The young warriors threw spears and fired poison darts at a helicopter of the Indian Coast Guard that tried, unsuccessfully, to recover the bodies. Such blind hostility to outsiders is clearly "maladaptive" in the modern world, but has served the Sentinelese well in the past, as it would have for all of our ancestors.

This isn't so far away from the blind and deadly animosity of the Bloods and Crips, notorious gangs of South Central Los Angeles who have been slaughtering one another for three decades. By tradition the Bloods wear red and the Crips wear blue. Both of these gangs have long and complex histories, and their conflict is in part driven by their natural rivalry in selling drugs and other criminal activities. But its intensity is clearly fueled by the deeper instincts associated with gang membership. The kids in each gang tend to be similar, growing up in the same kinds of neighborhoods, and facing the same kinds of problems. Many would naturally be friends, if not for their membership in opposing gangs. Indeed, I once read an interview (I cannot now recall where) in which the teenage members of one of these gangs were positively glowing in their praise for the courage and toughness of their enemies. "We have a lot of respect for those guys," one gang member said, "they're tough." Of course, he still had every intention of trying to kill those guys, because of the group to which they belonged—because of their colors.

Because of the primeval power of group bias, modern societies have laws, institutions, and social norms to curtail the most odious of its expressions. Yet its consequences remain evident everywhere, obvious in explicit racism and nationalism, less obvious elsewhere. A typical social phenomenon of "in group" behavior is heightened group allegiance and "rallying around" the leader in a time of crisis. On September 10, 2001, polls gave U.S. president George Bush among the lowest ratings of any modern president for that point in a first term. Only Gerald Ford, in the days and weeks following his extremely unpopular pardon of Richard Nixon, had comparable numbers. Following the attacks of 9/11, however, Bush's numbers immediately skyrocketed, with something like 90 percent of people thinking he was doing a good job. Bush supporters might like to see this as evidence of his strong leadership, but this is precisely the same pattern seen through history—national crises always boost a U.S. president's public support. When facing crises, people invariably see their leaders as strong almost regardless of the actions they take, feel more strongly connected to the group, and naturally become distrustful of outsiders and members of other groups. On May 2, 2006, the Montana State legislature finally offered an official pardon to seventy-nine U.S. citizens of German descent who, during the First World War, were convicted under a state law making it illegal to speak

German, to read or possess a book written in German, or to say or publish anything "disloyal, profane, violent, scurrilous, contemptuous or abusive" about the government or the American flag. One of those convicted and sentenced to seven to twenty years in the state penitentiary had done nothing more than call the organization behind the wartime food regulations "a big joke."[4]

What links all these examples, and almost any other instance of blind group loyalty or judgment, is the inflexibility of the behavior involved. People make decisions and take actions without investigation or considering other possibilities, as if following some basic channel along which they have been prepared and predisposed to think. In all these cases, people turn into primitives—it's us or them, Eagles or Rattlers. Of course, our instincts for group identification influence our lives at levels far less dramatic than ethnic hatred or gang warfare. In the run-up to the 2004 U.S. presidential election between George Bush and John Kerry, researchers led by psychologist Drew Westen of Emory University had partisan Republicans and Democrats look at quotes, from Bush or Kerry, in which the candidates were clearly contradicting themselves. Westen and colleagues monitored the brain activity in these individuals as they tried to explain the contradictions. They found no increased activity in parts of the brain normally engaged during reasoning. Rather, it was primarily brain circuits involved in emotion and conflict resolution that lit up. As Westen concluded, "None of the circuits involved in conscious reasoning were particularly engaged . . . Essentially, it appears as if partisans twirl the cognitive kaleidoscope until they get the conclusions they want." Many of us seem to filter reality in an emotional way so as to preserve and support a group to which we feel linked.

Where does this instinct come from? Primitive behavior, we shouldn't be surprised to learn, might make some primitive sense.

Indeed, this seems to be the case—although it takes some work on the computer to see why.

THE BRUTAL WISDOM OF PREJUDICE

A detailed examination of the causes and consequences of racism and nationalism could easily fill books; many such books exist already, of course. But to understand the roots of anything so pervasive in human life, we should first stand back from the details and ask if there might not be some simple and fundamental process at work. To do so, it helps to forget about the real world and, like Thomas Schelling with his coins, look first at an oversimplified world.

Imagine a world with some people in it who meet up with one another every so often to exchange goods, make business deals, and so on. We'll imagine in this model that each such encounter between two people is akin to the problem of the farmers, in which each person can benefit from the other's help, but also has the incentive to cheat. If people can learn to cooperate with one another, this would serve everyone, but it is easier said than done. Sticking your neck out to cooperate means opening yourself to being cheated. To make the problem really difficult for our people, and to make our world especially primitive, let's also suppose that the population is so huge that no two people ever meet one another for a second time, so it does no good to remember what someone has done in the past.

Obviously, this model isn't like our world. We normally assume that the deepest and most important differences among people lie in their personality, character, and intelligence, in their skills and experience. It's on the basis of these important traits that we generally try to learn about people and come to an informed decision about whom we can trust. In this model, as a thought experiment, we're supposing that none of this is possible, and clearly, in such a spare environment, in this informational desert, there's not a lot a person can do. You might try to cheat everyone you encounter, or to cooperate with everyone, or to act on a whim, being cooperating or cheating at random. There is no way to make a thinking strategy for any particular person because you know nothing about anyone you meet. Our thought experiment seems to show only that if people were all more or less identical bags of flesh, without memory and discernible character, we'd be drifting in social chaos, unable to form any enduring bonds of trust.

But this experiment becomes more informative if we make one tiny change. Suppose now that the people aren't all alike, but come in several colors—red, blue, green, and yellow. These color differences are completely arbitrary and meaningless—you might imagine that people get painted, randomly, at birth. Red people aren't any less likely to cooperate than blues, greens aren't born to be cheaters, and so on. But just because color is unimportant doesn't mean that some people might not think it makes a difference. For example, a yellow person, after interacting with fifteen different people, might notice that other yellows generally seem to be cooperative, while blues, greens, and reds seemed to cheat quite a lot. It would all be quite by accident, but this yellow person might decide that it is a good idea to cooperate with yellow people but not with anyone else. Other people, of course, may have different experiences. A blue may have been cheated three times running by other blues, while having great success cooperating with reds and greens, and decide that he should cooperate with other colors, but never with his own.

All of these people would be confused about the importance of color, which really has no importance at all. No matter. We've seen many times already how important patterns can emerge seemingly for no good reason at all, and this turns out to be the case here too, as political scientists Robert Axelrod and Ross Hammond discovered a few years ago. In becoming "color conscious," they reasoned, a person of this world could adopt one of four crude ways of thinking, choosing from a set of simple strategies. A person might come to think they should (1) cooperate with everyone, (2) cooperate with no one, (3) cooperate only with people of the same color, or (4) cooperate only with people of a different color.[5] They then asked a simple question: in the long run, will any one of these strategies do better than the others—that is, enable them to negotiate their interactions with others in a beneficial way?

To find out, Axelrod and Hammond devised a simple computer model of this artificial world. They spread the people out and had them interact in pairs and at random, with the natural stipulation that people living nearby to one another would be more likely to interact than those farther apart. People live and die, and occasionally they move from one place to another. The researchers started out with an equal number of all four colors and also doled out the four strategies in equal numbers, again at random. They also added in one other feature—the people in this world, like those in our world, can learn from the success of others.[6] So, if some yellow person sees that others who play strategy one tend to do better than those playing other strategies, they can begin using strategy one too. This is natural. Finally, Axelrod and Hammond let their computer run.

In a series of experiments, they let the artificial world evolve for a long time, until every individual had interacted with someone else at least a thousand times. Then they stopped the world to see what had happened. The results were always the same—

strategy number three, cooperate always but only with those of
your own color, had always spread through the population. In
the simulations, the researchers found that typically about three
fourths of all the agents eventually adopted this prejudiced strategy. Why? The answer is as simple as it is, quite possibly, profound.

Axelrod and Hammond found that out of the chaos of interactions, all determined quite at random, there emerges a natural
segregation of the population by color—you get enclaves of red,
others of blue or yellow. The success of the prejudiced strategy,
in fact, drives this segregation. At some point, by chance, a small
cluster of similarly colored, similarly prejudiced individuals will
form. In their interactions with one another, these people will do
well indeed—always cooperating. People located in the same region, but of another color, or having a nonprejudiced strategy,
won't do nearly so well, rarely getting any help from their prejudiced neighbors, and often wasting their efforts on others from
whom they get no reciprocation. Consequently, as individuals
look around, they see the prejudiced doing well, and the unprejudiced doing not so well. By learning, more people become
prejudiced. The real surprise, however, is that the overall level of
cooperation in this world also grows with time, even as people
become more prejudiced. As the homogeneous enclaves grow,
this brings most people (except those living at the boundaries
between different regions) to be nestled comfortably in a community of their own kind, amongst others of their color who
share their prejudice. They meet with cooperation in virtually all
their interactions. Because of the separation into enclaves, those
of different colors rarely have anything to do with one another.
Prejudice in this primitive world spreads because it works.[7]

In this primitive world, of course, "color" doesn't have to
mean color. It could refer to any kind of identifiable label that

could serve to tell people apart and to place them into groups—
it could be hair length, political affiliation, speaking accent, or
style of clothing. Whatever it may be, the logic shows that discrimination on the basis of meaningless labels can actually be a
powerful mechanism for producing cooperation. In effect, labels
put structure on an otherwise unstructured social reality and
thereby make it possible for people to make better decisions by
taking part in "tribes." What is really bizarre is that while these
labels are meaningless to begin with, they come to carry real
meaning. If you're an open-minded red person, even if you
know that people get painted at birth and are otherwise identical, you had better pay attention to color. Ultimately, most blue,
green, or yellow people won't cooperate with you, while other
reds will. In a world of bigots, only bigots survive.

In describing Hammond and Axelrod's work, I don't mean to
suggest that it offers the unique explanation of how ethnocentrism might have emerged. Indeed, anthropologists Peter Richerson and Robert Boyd of the University of California at Los
Angeles have developed a convincing alternative view in which
social norms play a role loosely akin to Hammond and Axelrod's
colors. But in its broad outlines, this view also makes the same
point—that prejudice, however ugly and damaging it may be,
likely has a very natural explanation as part of evolved behavior
that was adaptive for our ancestors. As these researchers argue,
people who share social norms generally find it easier to interact
positively as they share expectations about proper behavior. This
alone makes it easier to coordinate their activities and so realize
the benefits of cooperation. Indeed, Richerson and Boyd suggest
that the very existence of ethnicity itself—the emergence of stable groups defined by particular sets of "oughts" and "ought

nots" pertaining to dress, language, sexual behavior, and so on—
is ultimately linked to this coordinating advantage.[8]

No one would probably ever have identified this weird sorting process without the aid of a computer. No great social theorist or philosopher from Plato through Karl Marx to Émile
Durkheim ever spotted this logic, because the delicate trail of
cause and effect is simply beyond the power of the human mind.
It is also important to recognize, of course, that this cartoon
world is most certainly not our own world. So to see what this
model might imply, we need to think a little further.

THE ETHNOCENTRIC TRAP

Axelrod and Hammond's color game shows two remarkable
things. First, that when people interact in a primitive setting,
with only a few possible ways to try to get on in the interactions
with their neighbors, prejudice has an advantage. Prejudice, or
more accurately *ethnocentrism*, may be ugly, but at the most basic
level of human interaction, it is effective. Second, the rise of the
ethnocentric attitude and its spread through a population results,
surprisingly, in a more cooperative world. This is because ethnocentric behavior goes along with a spontaneous segregation of the
people into groups of specific colors, and so most interactions in
this primitive world come to be between people of the same color.
Replace color with "religion" or "nationality" or "language," and
you can easily see that something similar is true of our world too.

But this is all exceptionally abstract. To interpret this discovery
properly, we need to think a little more carefully about what it
might imply about the real world. Look at the social world around
you. Unless you're particularly unfortunate, you haven't lived in

violence-ravaged Darfur, where the Janjaweed, a militia group re-
cruited from local Arab tribes, is systematically wiping out the
non-Arab peoples of the region. Nor have you survived ethnic
cleansing in the former Yugoslavia, or experienced similar terror in
any of the other ethnic hot spots around the globe. If you're like
most people, you've experienced little that resembles the ethnocentric completeness of Axelrod and Hammond's world. In most
societies, fortunately, people of diverse religions, cultures, and languages cohabit in communities, join together in businesses, live as
friends and neighbors, and play games together. In the great cities,
New York or London, Mumbai or Mexico City, people of different cultures live in proximity and cooperate daily. Even in the former Yugoslavia, for many years, Croats, Serbs, and Muslims lived
peacefully in ethnically integrated communities, fulfilling the
dream of the Yugoslavian communist leader Marshal Tito. The
bare-bones model of ethnocentrism doesn't look much like this at
all. But, of course, that is part of the point—it shouldn't.

In most societies, and unlike in Axelrod and Hammond's
world, people interact as individuals rather than as mere repre-
sentatives of some racial, cultural, or otherwise labeled group.
They interact repeatedly because they live and work together,
they have memories and friends and form bonds of trust and understanding that undercut the potential power of such labels.
These other mechanisms for healthy social interaction—repeated
interactions between different types, strong institutions, and effective social norms—keep ethnocentrism at bay. The color game
shows what can happen, or will indeed happen, if people are
somehow forced to make decisions *only on the basis of crude and
superficial labels.* People under such conditions act on blind prejudice, because such prejudice works to their benefit. In effect, the
color game seems like a model of our world only under condi-

tions in which people are so stripped of their uniqueness and, through fear, coercion, brainwashing, or whatever, made unable to interact with other human beings as individual human beings. Strip away most of the ways we normally interact and build trust, the color game suggests, and you have a recipe for an ethnocentric trap. It does not result from a sickness of human character; indeed, it is not caused by anything foreign to human behavior at all. Ethnic division is a kind of universal tendency, like racial segregation, unless other prevailing forces keep it under control.

This cartoonlike artificial world, then, suggests that episodes of ethnic hatred and violence do really represent a kind of collapse into a more barbaric mode of human social organization. But the process cannot be understood by looking at the particular individuals involved, or their cultures, neither of which are inherently barbaric. It is, again, a question of pattern, not of people. Just as we'd all begin to make fires to stay warm if the vast systems that supply oil, gas, and electricity were suddenly destroyed, so people have to rely on more barbarous crude distinctions if the higher social mechanisms that support our peaceful togetherness get disrupted—which is precisely what many experts point to in the worst episodes of ethnic violence.

Social researchers see the primary cause of strong ethnic hatred as the breakdown of the normal social mechanics that let people form and maintain social bonds, across ethnic labels, by virtue of business, trade between communities, and so on. In the chaos of a collapsing economy, or in the midst of a civil war or revolution, a universe of dependable social interactions comes crashing down, and people resort to more primitive mechanisms for finding others to trust. Efforts to make sophisticated judgments of others' characters and reputations go out the window, and cruder impressions take their place. Outsiders and foreigners, those of another race, suddenly look more dangerous.

In the former Yugoslavia, the trouble began with wars in the breakaway republics of Slovenia and then Croatia, then moved to Bosnia. By then economic conditions had already deteriorated, as the country had for fifty years been heavily dependent on the Soviet Union. Militarized and treated as a satellite, it had never established a healthy economic infrastructure of its own. When the Soviet Union abruptly ceased to exist in 1987, the collapse of normal society brought more basic forces into play. And in this particular case, the raw materials, the ready labels required for ethnocentric division, were already in place as an ancient history of ethnic distrust had been capped by effective Soviet control.

But ethnic hatred and distrust do not have to lead to pillaging and violence. The conditions of social poverty are not enough to kick-start ethnic cleansing. A second common element in all genocidal events is the decisive action of some political leader or party that uses the dynamics of ethnic hatred for strategic ends, a process that goes beyond anything described in Axelrod and Hammond's color game. The American historian Henry Brooks Adams once suggested that practical politics, "whatever it professes, has always been about the systematic organization of hatreds." That may take things a little too far, but it touches an important point—that certain individuals can assert terrific power over human history, not because they are actually so powerful, intelligent, or charismatic as individuals, but because they are successful at manipulating social patterns.

OF MADMEN AND SOCIAL FORCES

Historians and philosophers of history have long argued about whether powerful individuals impose their wills upon the course of history, or whether history is instead determined by "social forces" of some less personal and more collective kind. Are nations driven to murderous wars by reckless, power-hungry leaders, or by deeper forces that are far greater than any one person? Historians once saw history as the "biography of great men." In more recent times, they have been more inclined to see economic forces, demographics, and broad cultural influences as the driving factors, rather than individual people. Which side is right? They both clearly have a point.

As Yugoslavia fell to pieces, and precisely as its multiethnic culture was most vulnerable to the divisive mind-set, Milosevic poured fuel onto the flames with a program of propaganda aimed at demonizing all non-Serbs and rallying the nation around a myth of Serbs as a suffering and oppressed people. In television and radio addresses, he portrayed the Croats as resurgent fascists from the Second World War, the Bosnian Muslims as bloodthirsty Ottoman Turks, and the Kosovo Albanians as killers seeking to wipe out the Serbs. In speeches, he motivated his Serbian paramilitaries by reminding them of the Turkish victory, and the "martyrdom" of Prince Lazar, at Blackbird's Field in 1389. As Czech political theorist Miroslav Hroch put it, Milosevic seized on nationalism as "a substitute for factors of integration in a disintegrating society."

In Rwanda, Armenia, or Nazi Germany, political leaders were clearly just as important in stirring up the trouble. In the lead-up to the Rwandan massacre, radio stations and newspapers owned by a handful of government officials began referring to the Tutsi as "subhuman." The government funded and organized radical Hutu groups that amassed weapons and trained people as killers. Plans for the impending genocide were even openly discussed in cabinet meetings. One minister said she was "personally in favor of getting rid of all Tutsi . . . without the Tutsi all of Rwanda's problems would be over." When, on April 6, 1994, Rwandan president Juvénal Habyarimana and the Hutu president of Burundi, Cyprien Ntaryamira, were killed when their plane was shot down in Kigali, the fate of 1 million Tutsis had virtually been sealed.[9]

Ethnic hatred doesn't become genocide without concerted and determined political action by an individual or a few individuals. This seems to suggest, in this one setting at least, that individuals can drive history. Then again, Slobodan Milosevic never had to shoot anyone. He may have been guilty, yet it seems difficult to attribute the deaths of tens of thousands, carried out by tens of thousands of other independent individuals, to any one person. Germany became Nazi Germany not only because of Hitler but because the temporary mood and character of the people in Germany made them ready to accept his message. History is controlled by the individual *and* the collective at once, and to see how this can be, more precisely, it helps again to think of patterns—and once again to consider physics.

It is true that the social world is made only of individuals, and only individuals make decisions and take actions. But speaking of history as only individuals is like talking about the ocean only in terms of molecules, while never mentioning waves. The unstoppable tsunami that struck Asia was nothing but molecules; yet it carried an immense destructive force in its coherence and collective organization. A wave is a pattern that organizes and channels the activity of many molecules and thereby gains inertia and momentum. The coherence of a wave acts back on and influences the molecules that make it up. Similarly, even if the social world is made only of individuals, social forces or patterns that involve thousands or millions act back on those individuals to constrain their choices, often in a way that reinforces the original pattern. In the case of ethnocentrism, the collective pattern, once it begins, has energy of its own. Even the most reasonable and tolerant become distrustful and capable of violence after repeated attacks from their neighbors.

The energy of the collective pattern gives individuals, such as Milosevic, the ability to wield immense power, precisely by understanding the logic of the pattern and being able to direct it for his own ends. Slobodan Milosevic could have been born in a thousand other settings and never influenced as many lives as he did. He could be a powerful force for evil because he understood, intuitively or intellectually, the collective forces at work in his nation. Anyone who stirs up huge social currents, from great statesmen to unspeakable dictators, does so by using their actions to give form to and direct the movement of far larger energies than they possess individually. But this also means they do not push things solely by their will, but must conform and find their possibilities outlined by the laws of social physics.

In this regard, it is also interesting to think about the hierarchical organization of our societies, which puts a few people in positions of great power. One may suppose that these people have made it into these positions because of their greatness, in which one can see the actions of any leader as reflecting the power of individuals to drive history. A somewhat deeper view should, however, seek to explain why we have hierarchical organization in the first place. It is clear historically, from primitive tribes organized around one chief or "big man" through to modern societies, that a group is more capable insofar as it can organize the actions of anything from hundreds to millions of people into a coherent and coordinated form. Hierarchical organization is one effective way to do this, as a person in the position of power can, with a few words, direct the energies of the many. But to attribute great power to that individual is a mistake. The collective has organized itself in such a way as to give one person lots of power, because the collective itself is then more powerful and able to adapt. Again, the individual's power stems from the collective organization, rather than their special greatness as a person.

So the lesson of social physics, if you will, is that ethnic hatred is a primitive "mode" of human collective behavior, akin to the natural vibrations of a guitar string or the swinging of a pendulum. If this weren't the case, stoking ethnic hatred would never be an effective political strategy, as it would push against human tendency and inclination. Politicians play to ethnic fears because they know fear motivates, perhaps, more basically and immediately than any other emotion. And, in the right setting, the opportunistic intelligence of a power-hungry individual can control the actions of millions.

THE SIMPLE STORY

It may seem presumptuous to suggest that something as complicated as ethnic warfare, which depends on the wills and actions of millions of people, ruins countless lives, and stands at the extreme of human experience, might really have quite a lot to do with something as simple as Axelrod and Hammond's color game. People are complicated, the social world is complicated, cultures are complicated, and they stretch through history. So it seems unlikely that an almost trivial mathematical model could go very far in explaining how they work. If you have this suspicion, then you share it with many people and with an entire tradition in social science. But this objection rests on a myth about science, and a deep misunderstanding of the importance and possibility of getting to the core of complicated things with extremely simplified models. That this would be possible may seem like a scientific miracle. Perhaps it is. But without such miracles, there would be no science at all.

Physics is often called an "exact" science. But if physicists work with equations and try to find exact solutions to those equations, conceptually, philosophically, and in practice the strength of physics always rests on the art of making approximations—of learning to ignore details that don't really matter, and to focus only on those that do. I think, if we physicists are honest, we don't really know, except in some special cases, why we are able to do this—to learn so much while relying on such vastly oversimplified pictures of reality. The universe seems to have cut us a break; the world seems to be put together in a way that is simpler than it might have been.

Consider an iron magnet of the kind you attach to the refrigerator. Magnets do seemingly magical things, such as sticking to refrigerators, or tugging on nails. But if you heat the magnet in a furnace to a temperature of 770 degrees, you'll find that magnet suddenly loses its power and no longer tugs on nails. Take it out, and the magic returns. Remarkably, physicists only learned the crude story behind this transformation about a century ago and only came to a detailed theory in the last several decades. Recall that in chapter 5 we pictured iron atoms as microscopic magnets, akin to tiny arrows. At room temperature, these arrows push and pull on one another and tend to line up. Through their teamwork, they can pull on nails.[10] What happens in the furnace? Temperature is a measure of the vigor of disorganized atomic motion. At high temperatures, the natural jostling of the atoms makes the arrows bounce and flutter and have difficulty staying in line. At 770°C, a magnet loses its magnetic power because the arrows lose their ability to stay in line—the organization gets destroyed.

The mathematical details of how this organization dissolves actually represent a beautiful area of modern physics. Modern theories based on this picture of "tiny arrows" produce impressively accurate predictions of how the change takes place. (The theory of "phase transitions," of which this is a part, is also a source of ideas fundamental to almost every branch of physics, from string theory to cosmology.) But the most amazing thing, and the reason I am mentioning this, is that the accuracy of the explanation is in no way tied to the accuracy of the physical picture, which is, in fact, a shocking abuse of reality. An iron atom is extremely complicated. It contains a nucleus of twenty-six protons and thirty neutrons surrounded by a cloud of twenty-six electrons. Each of the protons and neutrons is itself made of quarks flying around at speeds approaching that of light, and the electrons interact with one another in ways that no one fully understands. To be faithful to reality, a theory should treat all of this within the framework of quantum theory. The exact equations would be difficult even to write down, and far beyond the capacity of a mathematical genius to solve.

But no matter—physicists have learned that you can leave out quantum theory, forget about all those neutrons and protons, electrons and quarks, and just pretend that atoms are little arrows. This gives an unbelievably accurate picture of the way a magnet works. If this seems like a miracle, it is, but the key, it seems, is that the model of "tiny arrows" does get right what really matters—it pays attention to the fact that every atom has a direction associated with it, and that one atom exerts a force on others that tends to make them line up. The transition from magnet to nonmagnet is all about a change in organization, and the way this takes place doesn't depend sensitively on many details. The point isn't that any oversimplified model will do, but that oversimplified models can go a long way *if they get right the few details that really matter.*

All good science depends on "miracles" of this general kind—on the fact that the important patterns rarely depend sensitively on thousands of factors, but on only a crucial few. For this reason, science doesn't need exact models that try to capture reality in all its gory and infinite detail. We need to work in precisely the opposite direction, by ignoring everything we possibly can and making theories as simple as possible. The seemingly trivial logic of some "toy" model doesn't preclude it from striking right at the heart of real-world happenings, even if they do involve people.

Chapter 8

CONSPIRACIES AND NUMBERS

> *The general public has long been divided into two*
> *parts: those who think that science can do anything,*
> *and those who are afraid it will.*
>
> —DIXY LEE RAY (AMERICAN MINISTER)

O N   T H E   M O R N I N G of August 19, 1942, more than six
thousand Allied troops, mostly Canadian, carried out a
surprise raid on the French port city of Dieppe. The raid was the
first Allied attempt to wrest the initiative back from the German
military machine after its spectacular success in Europe and in
North Africa; it was also an unmitigated disaster. When the main
attack hit the Dieppe beachfront, German troops met it with an
uncompromising barrage of artillery and machine-gun fire that
pinned troops to the beach. By early afternoon, 907 Canadians
were dead and the Germans had taken 1,946 prisoners of war.
Only 2,210 of the 4,963 Canadians who embarked on the operation were able to return to England.

The raid at Dieppe failed largely for straightforward military
reasons. The German troops were well prepared, and taking even
a lightly defended port city turned out to be far more difficult

than Allied planners had thought. They never tried it again during the war. But in England, days later, these mundane facts took second place to a more fantastic explanation. According to rumor, a radio advertisement for a home soap product, Sylvan soap flakes, had referred to the Dieppe beach several days before the raid. As rumors often do, this one suggested a comforting possibility—that a spy had signaled the place and time of the attack to the Germans, who therefore had an unfair advantage. Though false, this conspiratorial rumor offered a psychologically attractive alternative to a frightening truth—that the catastrophe largely reflected the Allies' inexperience and the superior skill and force of their enemy.[1]

Conspiratorial explanations persist because they suggest interpretations that seem safer or psychologically more acceptable; they often attribute evil doings to one's natural enemies or show how some surprising happening actually fits in with a predetermined view of how the world works. When it comes to cooking up conspiratorial explanations, the human mind has no apparent limits. A semipopular theory still getting attention holds that HIV, the virus that causes AIDS, did not naturally evolve but was engineered by the U.S. Defense Department and released in a targeted attack on gays, Africans, and drug users. According to a CNN poll conducted across nine Muslim countries in February 2002, 61 percent of those polled believed that Arabs were not behind the attacks of 9/11; that it was instead perpetrated by the Israeli security services or the U.S. government itself. An American "UFO researcher" named William Cooper has for many years insisted that the Secret Service itself carried out the 1963 assassination of U.S. president John F. Kennedy after he threatened to reveal publicly that the U.S. government had already signed treaties with at least three distinct races of space aliens.[2]

But conspiratorial thinking isn't always so obviously tinged with elements of the crazy and implausible. In a more mundane and ordinary way, it finds its way, for example, into the discourse of everyday politics. Wealth in the United States is not distributed evenly across the population. Currently, about 85 percent of all the wealth rests in the hands and bank accounts of the top 20 percent of households.[3] What is the cause of this inequity? The political left and right, of course, have ready explanations. For those on the left, the degree of inequality can only reflect an inherent flaw in free market capitalism, which gives a wealthy few the power to control the many. For those on the right, on the contrary, the wealthy have earned their position only through skill and hard work and deserve every penny. The only thing that unites these arguments, of course—and unfortunately typifies most political discourse—is the complete triumph of conviction over evidence. As with the more obvious conspiracy theories, conclusions take the stage first and go searching for justification later.

To be really useful, the science of the human world has to go beyond stories of this kind. Doing so means doing what all con- spiracy thinking doesn't do, and what science does, which is to test speculations by careful comparison with reality. As the philosopher of science Karl Popper argued, scientific theories, to have any value, have to be "falsifiable"—they must make specific claims that can be checked and that might, in principle, turn out to be wrong. In physics, a theory gains respect by sticking its neck out—by making specific predictions about patterns that we should find in the world. If it is wrong, the theory's head gets lopped off. If right, then the idea gains status as seemingly on the right track, and therefore worthy of further exploration.

Early in this book I suggested that the ideas of social physics, by recognizing the importance of pattern, feedback, and self-organization in the social world, are beginning to make this kind of science possible for the human world. We saw two examples of specific mathematical patterns in chapters 4 and 5, in market fluctuations and in the changes of fashions or opinions. In the two most recent chapters, I've stepped away from mathematics a little and looked qualitatively at how simple models can be extremely powerful in helping to elucidate the kinds of surprising effects that follow out of routine human behaviors. But in this chapter, I'd like to return to the idea of mathematical laws for the social world, starting with the puzzle of wealth inequality itself—which turns out, when viewed from the right perspective, to have a fairly simple explanation.

HUMAN UNIVERSALS

When anthropologists talk about "human universals," they mean habits of individual behavior or social activity that turn up again and again, across cultures and continents. As anthropologist Donald Brown of the University of California at Santa Barbara puts it, human universals are "those features of culture, society, language, behavior, and mind that, so far as the record has been examined, are found among all peoples known to ethnography and history."[4] People of all cultures use tools and follow daily routines, speak a language with grammar, and capture key elements of human experience in myths and legends. All people use gestures and facial expressions and have recourse to psychological defense mechanisms, in handling fear and in managing grief, for example. At the social level, all human groups without exception have evolved means for organizing the division of labor and getting people to work together.

Other universals, though not quite so obvious, run just as deep.

One might anticipate that the way a nation's wealth is divided among its people should depend on lots of details about the people and nation in question. You might expect the laws of inheritance and taxation to matter a great deal, and also the nature of the country's major economic activity, be it in agriculture, heavy industry, or what have you. You'd expect culture to matter also, as some people place more importance on social equality than others. But the numbers show that all these expectations are actually way off base—the distribution of wealth, worldwide, has a remarkable universal character. As Italian economist Vilfredo Pareto noted more than a century ago, in all nations you find that a small fraction of the wealthiest people always possesses a lion's share of a country's riches. In the United States only 20 percent of the people possess 85 percent of the wealth, and the numbers are similar in Chile, Bolivia, Japan, South Africa, or the nations of Western Europe. It might be 10 percent owning 90 percent, 5 percent owning 85 percent, or 3 percent owning 96 percent, but in all cases, wealth seems to migrate into the hands of the few. Indeed, although good data is sadly lacking, studies in the mid-1970s based on interviews with Soviet emigrants even suggested that wealth inequality in the communist Soviet Union was then comparable to that of the UK.[5]

But Pareto actually discovered something a little deeper than this qualitative similarity across nations. Digging into the mathematics, he found that the distribution of wealth in all nations turns out to follow one basic mathematical form. Specifically, if you look at the wealthier part of the population, you will always find that the number of people having wealth, W, is inversely proportional to W^α, where α is a number around two and one-half; in other words, the number of people falls off as the wealth raised to a power between two and three. Intriguingly, this is precisely the same pattern—a so-called power law—that we met in chapter 4 for fluctuations in financial markets. What it means in this case is that each time wealth goes up by a factor of ten, the number of people having that much falls by a factor of about six (about six times as many people have $1 million, for example, as have $10 million). The numbers dwindle in a natural and regular way.

This human universal goes well beyond mere qualitative similarities among people, their tool use, ability for language, their strategic skills for managing cooperative relations with others. Countless studies since Pareto's time have confirmed this regularity across continents and cultures. It provides a dramatic illustration of how our individual actions, despite our free will and the 15 million things that people get up to, can still lead to mathematical regularities every bit as precise as those found in physics. What causes this striking regularity across nations? Does it simply reflect the natural distribution of human talent? Or, is there some devilish conspiracy among the rich? Not surprisingly, given the strong emotions stirred by matters of wealth and its disparity, economists in the past have flocked to such questions. As economist John Kenneth Galbraith noted in his history of the field, "The explanation and rationalization of the resulting inequality has commanded some of the greatest, or in any case some of the most ingenious, talent in the economics profession."[6]

But it is also true that no generally accepted explanation has been forthcoming—until recently.[7]

As it turns out, finding a legitimate explanation means getting past all those details that common sense tells us should matter, from differences in individual talent to inheritance and the influence of powerful social connections, and beginning to think of wealth more crudely as if it were a kind of physical substance. It flows around from person to person. Sometimes it gets created or destroyed. Focusing on this basic picture, and taking into account just a little of the character of the social atom, appears to be enough to resolve the mystery.

MONEY MATTERS

A person's wealth, by definition, is everything he or she owns, from a car to a house to the canned goods in their cupboards, plus their bank accounts and any stocks and bonds, and finally minus all their debts. Every one of us has a certain amount of wealth, some more than others, and these amounts bounce up and down over time as we get paid, spend money, or as stocks soar or plummet. Making predictions about how any one person's wealth will wax and wane over time is certainly a tricky matter. But from the simplest conceivable standpoint, we can say a few things with confidence about how a person's wealth can change—logically speaking, there are two different and equally fundamental ways.

The average annual pay for workers in the United States is now around $30,000. Every year, companies transfer this amount on average to each of their employees. Of course, that money came from somewhere, usually out of the hands of other people who bought the goods or services those companies provide. This is the first way that wealth changes—by flowing between people. Every time cash changes hands, you deposit a check, or buy a gift with a credit card, a little wealth trickles along the links of economic exchange, making one person a little more wealthy and another a little less. Transactions of this sort form the bread and butter of our daily economic lives, as individuals gain or lose wealth, even though the total amount remains the same.

But a second way that individual wealth can change doesn't leave the total fixed—through investment. During the 1990s, stocks in technology and especially Internet companies climbed by a factor of five, creating an enormous value for stockholders (on paper at least) that wasn't there before. As I am writing this, U.S. housing prices are beginning to tumble after a spectacular rise over the past decade. Investments often create wealth. Of course, they can also erase it. Although many people seem convinced that housing prices always rocket upward, they have plummeted on numerous occasions, and may do so again, much as Internet stocks did in the spring of 2000. Investment is the second way our wealth can change, and it depends heavily on an element of chance.

If we think of wealth as a substance, then we see that it flows from person to person, and sometimes, when in one person's hands and he or she invests it, its amount changes, getting bigger or smaller. Rather unexpectedly, this simple picture, combined with one further insight into human behavior, explains Vilfredo Pareto's discovery.

Several years ago, physicists Jean-Philippe Bouchaud and Marc Mezard began exploring the workings of an artificial world based around these facts.[8] In this world, people would exchange wealth by making transactions with others and also gain and lose it through investments. To make their social atoms behave realistically, the physicists also assumed one thing further—that the value of wealth is relative. A single parent trying to work and raise her son might face near ruin over the loss of $100; in contrast, a rich person wouldn't flinch after losing a few thousand. In other words, the value of a little more or less wealth depends on how much one already has. This implies that when it comes to investing, wealthy people will tend to invest proportionally more than the less wealthy. (Few of the poor own stocks, for example.) Using a computer, Bouchaud and Mezard simulated the workings of an artificial economy made up of a large number of "people" leading their economic lives according to these rules, making exchanges and investments. They quickly found that transactions between people tend to spread wealth around. If one person becomes terrifically wealthy, he or she may travel, build houses, and consume more products, and in each case wealth will tend to flow out to others. Likewise, a poor person will purchase fewer products, and less wealth will flow away from them. Overall, the flow of funds between people tends to wash away wealth disparities. However, this washing-out turns out to be no match for a countervailing force.

Although they gave everyone in their artificial work exactly equal skill at choosing investments, Bouchaud and Mezard found that pure luck caused some people to accumulate more wealth than others. These people then had more wealth to invest, gaining a chance to get still more. And this brings us to the real secret of our inability to understand wealth inequality—our lack of appreciation for how rapidly gains that multiply on themselves become large. Take a piece of whisper-thin paper, say about 0.1 mm thick. Now suppose you fold it in half twenty-five times in a row, doubling its thickness each time. How thick will it be? Almost everyone asked such a question will grossly underestimate the result. In this case, the folded paper would be about twenty miles thick. Similarly, a string of positive investment returns, because it builds a person's wealth not merely by addition but by multiplication, is enough to stir up huge wealth disparities in the population. The result, in the model, is that most of the wealth automatically accumulates in the hands of a small minority. What's more, the mathematical distribution across people follows precisely the same power law seen in reality.

Given the simplicity of the assumptions going into Bouchaud

and Mezard's model, and the precise agreement of the outcome with real-world numbers, it is hard to argue with the conclusion of this study. Inequality seems to have nothing to do with the ready answers of the political right or left. As the wealth game illustrates by example, a completely natural process can push most of the wealth into the hands of a minority without any conspiracy or collusion by the powerful. It also shows that you should expect enormous differences in wealth regardless of the distribution of human talent; you'd find them even if all people were exactly equal in their moneymaking skills. So you cannot infer that the wealthy have their wealth simply because of their intelligence or hard work.

This insight resonates with the finding of many studies suggesting that enormous differences in human achievement often arise from simple logical processes, rather than innate differences in skill.[9] To take one example, Mikhail Simkin and Vwani Roychowdhury of the University of California recently took a second look at the spectacular flying record of First World War ace Manfred von Richthofen, aka the Red Baron. Richthofen chalked up eighty consecutive victories in aerial combat, a record that would seem to reflect exceptional skill, as such a tally is unlikely to be attributed to pure luck. But maybe not. Simkin and Roychowdhury studied the records of all German fighter pilots of the First World War and found a total of 6,745 victories, but only about 1,000 "defeats," which included fights in which pilots were killed or wounded. As they point out, the imbalance reflects, in part, that fighter pilots often scored easy victories against poorly armed or less maneuverable aircraft, making the average German fighter pilot's rate of success as high as 80 percent. This is significant because, statistically speaking, there is then a pretty fair chance that at least one of the nearly three thousand German pilots active during the war would have won eighty aerial fights in a row by pure chance. The analysis also suggested that while von Richthofen and other aces were in the upper 30 percent of pilots by skill, they were probably no more special than that. The authors concluded that "the top aces achieved their victory scores mostly by luck."[10]

The wealth game doesn't include any details of a particular country or its people and isn't meant to supply the definitive account for the United States, Germany, Britain, Colombia, or any other nation. But this is just the point—the process described is, like Schelling's segregation game, so fundamental, and works at a level so far beneath those details, that it has to be a large part of the answer about what goes on in any country.[11] This basic understanding helps us to step back from certain political arguments, and shows once again that simple forces working behind the scenes can lead to social outcomes having a lawlike mathematical form. But there is a further point—that none of this, in the context of modern science, should really come as a surprise. The universal law of wealth inequality merely illustrates a profound resonance between the mathematical laws of the human world and those for the rest of nature.

RIVERS ON MARS

The Mississippi River plunges into the Gulf of Mexico after winding southward through Middle America, where tributaries branch off haphazardly to the east and west. The irregularity is little surprise because the specific layout of any river network reflects the geophysical history of the region, including earthquakes that shifted the river's course, patterns of rainfall, and so on. The overall structure of the river and its branches is like a fingerprint of this place on earth and its history. But behind this irregularity, perhaps in spite of it, the network of all streams and smaller rivers that ultimately feed into the Mississippi, like all such networks, possesses a surprising organization.

The amount of water that any particular branch of a river network carries reflects the size of its "catchment area," the total land area that drains into it. Near the Gulf of Mexico, the Mississippi is quite large, as it drains the water from most of the western and midwestern United States. Moving northward and upstream, the river and its entering tributaries get narrower because they drain smaller areas. Remarkably, this progression toward narrower and more numerous river segments follows a precise mathematical pattern. You might think of the larger rivers, those carrying lots of water, as being the "richer" ones, and the smaller rivers as being "poorer." Thinking in such terms, if you then go and count up how many rivers there are of all sizes (size measured by total water flow), you would find, as many studies have, that the number of rivers falls off with increasing size and in an exceptionally regular way. Specifically, the number of rivers with an amount W of water flowing through them (say, per day) is proportional to $1/W^\alpha$, where α is about 1.43.[12] This should look vaguely familiar, because this is the same basic mathematical form that describes the way wealth falls among people (the precise value of the number α has changed, but the form is the same). Oddly enough, water flows through river segments in pretty much the same way that wealth accumulates in the hands of people.

So the layout of the Mississippi and its network of tributaries isn't quite as haphazard as it looks. But there is more to the story. If you went on to study other rivers, you'd find the same pattern for the Yangtze in China, the Nile in Egypt, and the Volga in Russia. In fact, geophysicists have found this pattern in every river they've ever studied, revealing that a hidden organization lies behind their disorderly and often very different appearances. This universal power law for river networks reflects a regularity that is a modern relative of the pattern that Kepler discovered for the orbits of the planets, if only a little more subtle. Modern geophysicists have played the role of Newton and found a theory that explains this regularity. Roughly speaking, it comes down to feedback, as the flow of water causes erosion, which alters the shape of the terrain, which in turn alters how the water flows, and so on. A few simple equations capture the process, just as a few simple equations capture the flow and multiplication of wealth in an economy, leading to a few rich and many poor.

I've mentioned river networks not because they teach us anything directly about the human world, but because it is more than accidental that the same mathematical regularity turns up in two very different settings. These regularities, which I have called power laws, are relationships in which one quantity, A, is proportional to another, B, taken to some power n; that is, $A \sim B^n$. Aside from wealth and river-drainage basins, trees, clouds, and fractured surfaces all conform to power laws, as do fluctuations in Internet traffic, the response of the immune system, and a vast range of other natural phenomena. Power laws also arise in the statistics of events that would seem to be utterly random, such as earthquakes and forest fires. For example, the number of earthquakes that release energy, E—a measure of their strength—is simply proportional to $1/E^2$.[13]

These findings reflect a simplicity that lurks behind complexity, and they hold fundamental importance for modern science. For a century or more, physics has focused principally on systems in "equilibrium"; indeed, virtually everything we know about the properties of ordinary substances, from metals to liquid crystals, from semiconductors to superfluids, rests on equilibrium theories. So do many of the more "exotic" applications of physics to such areas as quantum computation. In sharp contrast, power laws emerge naturally in systems that are decidedly not in equilibrium, such as the earth's crust or the Internet, which evolve perpetually and never settle into an unchanging state. Attempts to build theories for this huge and largely unexplored area of "nonequilibrium" systems, with applications in physics, chemistry, and biology, but also in other settings, such as economics, now go by the name "complexity science." One of its primary discoveries is that finding lawlike patterns in complex nonequilibrium systems generally means taking a step back from the details, and focusing on the larger picture. We cannot predict accurately which person will be rich and which poor, or how large the next earthquake will be. The lawlike and predictable patterns emerge instead at the level of many events, in the statistics. This insight, unfortunately, has yet to make many waves in the human sciences.

Taking this step back from the prediction of particulars to more general patterns doesn't mean giving up the ability to answer important questions. A few years ago, NASA's *Mars Orbiter* satellite passed closely over Mars and took detailed images of its surface, mapping hills and valleys and ridges. Italian physicist Guido Caldarelli and colleagues took this data, in digital form, and traced out a network of interlocking valleys that, to the human eye, *looks* like an archaic river network. It's dry now, however, so it is not clear that this is really the case. But the physicists looked at the statistical character of the branches of this network and found that it follows precisely the same power law as rivers on Earth. The mathematical correspondence offers convincing proof that the topography of this part of Mars was created by the same process that creates river networks on Earth—the flowing of liquid under the forcing of gravity.[14]

ISLANDS OF COOPERATION

Philosophers and economists since the time of Adam Smith (and even well before) have marveled at the power of the "market" to help people organize their economic activities. Beneath the hype, there really is something quite impressive about how markets use collective social activity to make us smarter, as individuals, than we would otherwise be. In this sense, as the economist Friedrich von Hayek once argued, it is not so much the rationality of people that makes the market effective, but the effectiveness of the market that makes us more rational. I don't have the slightest idea, really, of what it costs in labor, materials, and otherwise to produce anything from a new pair of jeans to a packet of mozzarella cheese. But I can purchase these things, and not pay too much over the odds, because the market has worked the price out for me. The independent action of many people, both buyers and sellers, brings prices to about the right level.

But Hayek's argument, and the common rhetoric of free market superiority, also points to a deeper puzzle. If the free market is so great, why isn't everything the free market? Or, to look at it another way, why are there business firms? From bagels and pillowcases to investment services, almost everything we use is produced by people working together in some company, from a two-person bagel outfit to General Electric. Within a firm, and unlike the free market, people don't pursue their own ends but follow a coordinated plan that comes down from above. Why don't workers and managers negotiate their interactions in offices plastered with advertisements for this or that worker's "excellent skills" and "low, low prices"? Why does the free market rule outside of a firm's boundaries, but not inside? Free market enthusiasts like to celebrate the power of the marketplace over "central planning," as in the former Soviet Union and other communist countries. But paradoxically, as economist Hal Varian of the University of California has put it, "the primary unit of capitalism, on close inspection, looks a lot like central planning."[15]

Of course, it is quite naïve to believe that anything as rich as human economic life can be summed up with a platitude such as "the market is always best." It isn't, and for good reason. Long ago, economist Ronald Coase pointed out that activity in the free market isn't quite as "free" as we usually think it is. If you buy a new car, you will pay more for it than whatever the value of the check you eventually write out. To begin with, you'll have to spend time visiting dealers, looking through newspapers, and reading *Consumer Reports.* Once you find a car and a seller, you then have to haggle for a good price. Any sale or other exchange has some hidden "transaction costs" that do not ordinarily get written down in the accountant's ledger. Businesses routinely hire expensive lawyers to write contracts that will enforce the terms of their exchanges. Coase argued that firms exist, at least in part, to reduce these hidden costs that make the free market more expensive than it seems. Within a firm, people share skills and make exchanges without such worries, because management exerts top-down control.

This is the story as usually told, but there is another way to look at it. Most of us, even working in companies and under the boss's control, ultimately make our own decisions. We could quit, and people routinely enter and leave firms of their own accord. The free market does exist. The question is how is it that the workings of the free market naturally lead to the emergence of something that looks like central planning—to the firm? Groups of people banding together to reduce transaction costs is part of the story, but it is not the whole story.

A few years ago, sociologist Robert Axtell of the Brookings Institution in Washington, D.C., undertook a statistical analysis of the more than 5 million commercial enterprises then operating in the United States. Looking at the number of firms of different sizes—as reflected by their total sales, S—he found a striking power law pattern: the number of firms having total sales, S, is simply proportional to $1/S^2$. This means that firms with sales of $1 million are precisely four times as numerous as those with $2 million, which are in turn four times as numerous as those with $4 million, and so on, right across the board. Think of this for a moment. Millions of people with infinitely varied interests and skills have joined together into firms—some just for the money, some to carry on a family business, and so on. These firms do everything from washing cars or walking dogs to making cruise missiles. But out of all this chaos emerges a mathematical pattern of amazing simplicity. It is as if the U.S. government had worked out targets and somehow enforced its plan with unprecedented bureaucratic efficiency.[16]

As we saw in the story of water on Mars, an accurate law of this kind can be a tool for investigation. Any kind of theory that would hope to explain the firm had better reproduce this simple pattern. But it had better get some other things right too. As it turns out, the growth rates of firms also follow another power law—they fluctuate less among larger firms than among smaller ones, and, again, in a precise mathematical way.[17] Any acceptable theory should also account naturally for the way firms continually come and go. Although General Motors and Microsoft and Exxon seem like permanent features of the economic landscape, they cannot be too comfortable. Less than half of the largest five thousand U.S. firms in 1980 now exist. Finally, of course, such a theory should do all this while remaining faithful to what we know about the social atom as an adaptive, goal-oriented creature.

This may seem like a tall order. No traditional theory of economics has ever come close, and this is no great surprise, as economics has long been fixated on an unrealistically static and equilibrium picture of the world.[18] But finding a much better theory isn't so hard. It just means coming to grips with the real consequences of our incentives for working together and cooperating, and the unavoidable problems associated with doing so effectively.

COOPERATION AND ITS DISCONTENTS

Anyone who has read the preceding chapters can just about guess what is coming next. It is an important subtheme of this book that the complex, even in the human world, often finds its roots in the simple. This particular puzzle unfolds in a familiar way. Much of what we know about the real economic world—including the mathematical patterns just described—tumble out of a terrifically oversimplified picture of the working world formed around ideas so basic that they seem beyond dispute. Get right the workings of the essential parts, and the rest follows.

Imagine a working world stripped of nearly all its details, without executives flying around the globe, without PalmPilots and expense accounts, and based around just three basic features that reflect the absolute core of working reality. First, there are lots of people in this world and each can choose to work on his or her own or can join together and work with others in some company.

Second, because of teamwork and cooperation, working together has the *potential* to bring these individuals benefits. A successful firm of ten people, for example, generally produces more than ten times a single person's output, and employees share in this benefit by making more money than they would on their own. This is an obvious element of the business world, but a third element is just as obvious—that getting people to cooperate and continue cooperating isn't easy because of the perpetual threat of cheating. As we know, "free riding" can undermine group cooperation. In the work setting, clever and selfish people may skimp on their own effort while still taking their share of the group's overall productivity. So being part of a firm is no guarantee of high earnings—you might well end up carrying the load for an office full of slackers and do worse than you could on your own.

The interplay of these few factors leads to an extremely rich dynamic that does really seem to explain the nature of firms. Several years ago, Axtell programmed a computer to follow an artificial economy in which individuals could come together into firms. To start off, all were working on their own, but they could change their minds and join with others if that would bring them more income. To make the model just slightly more detailed, Axtell also included some personality differences—some people were ambitious and hardworking, with a high demand for income, while others were less ambitious and could accept less to have more free time. At first, Axtell found that because hardworking individuals produce more together than when apart, this is indeed what happened: ambitious types began to gather together into firms. As time went on, firms grew, became more productive, and attracted more employees, both ambitious and less ambitious. This was the prelude to a more intricate story.

In a small firm, each person's effort has a large impact on the total output, so what a worker gets out depends on what he or she puts in. In small firms, therefore, no one has the incentive to free ride; all have the incentive to work hard. In a large firm, however, any one person's contribution to the overall effort becomes much smaller. So if someone doesn't really put in much effort, but only pretends to work hard, he or she will still get just as much because the overall productivity of the company will barely suffer. In Axtell's simulations, he found that the growing size of some firms indeed induced some individuals, usually the less ambitious, to begin cheating. Unfortunately, their example soon spread as hard workers, discontented by seeing their efforts pay off not for themselves, but for the slackers, also began shirking. Axtell made it possible for individuals to leave firms or switch between them, if they could find a better situation. The computer showed that large firms, once infected with free riders, suffer in a characteristic way—by losing their hard workers to other firms with fewer free riders or to begin work on their own.

In short, firms grow out of cooperation and the benefits it brings, but their success sets the stage for later cheating, which undermines the cooperation on which the firm depends. The result is not equilibrium or anything like it, but a perpetual churning as new companies of hard workers form, grow larger and older, eventually become infected by free riding, and then suffer the consequences. What makes it all much more than a toy is that it reproduces what we see in reality with astonishing accuracy. In the simulations, the distribution of firms by size quickly settles on a fixed and unchanging form, with firm size (measured either in number of employees or output) following a power law like that observed in reality. More remarkably, the power law for growth rates also falls out of the process, as does another power law for the distribution of firm lifetimes. By starting from utter simplicity, but trusting in the power of simple rules to generate complexity, this computer model has explained patterns that no economic theory ever has.[19]

This mathematical success gives us a rock-solid reason for thinking that this picture of what drives firms really is on the right track. And it suggests an unusual, though in hindsight perhaps not surprising, take on the business world. We usually think of business as favoring the "ruthless" and the "hard-nosed," those skilled in "cutthroat" decision making and "take no prisoners" competition. The clichés are endless. But it instead appears that at the core of the modern competitive firm we find that social cohesion created by cooperation is the main engine of success. Companies that succeed for long periods do so by sustaining the cooperative spirit in their employees and therefore gaining from their hard work. At the center of the modern firm, paradoxically, we find the same precious resource for social function that helped out hunter-gatherer ancestors one hundred thousand years ago.

CAUSALITY AND CHANCE

By 700 BC, the Babylonians had developed skill in predicting lunar eclipses; they understood their world better than earlier peoples. Over the next twenty-five hundred years, science honed its ability to make accurate predictions, with Galileo, Kepler, and finally Isaac Newton bringing the world's mechanistic predictability to center stage. In the Newtonian universe, as Pierre-Simon Laplace pointed out, a being of sufficient intelligence could predict the future in detail by knowing the positions and velocities of all particles at any moment. Today, science uses the term *prediction* more casually. One might predict that a new material will be superconducting below 40 K, or that a mouse lacking a certain gene will also lack a particular trait. Such predictions always precede their experimental test, yet aim less to foretell the future than to explore scientific understanding. Prediction in this sense is the engine of science: we design the present (the experiment) and observe the future (the result) so as to compare our theories with empirical reality.

What we have seen in the examples of this chapter is that modern science is now progressing toward a further refinement of the notion of prediction. We cannot predict with certainty when a child is born how much wealth he or she will eventually have. Too many accidents enter into things; the thousands of relevant factors make prediction impossible. Likewise, we cannot predict with any certainty how long a company such as Amazon or eBay will exist. But even when prediction of such specific details is impossible, it may be possible to make predictions, even precise mathematical predictions, about the statistics that emerge and hold for many such events. As we saw with wealth inequality and also with the size of firms, mathematical regularities in the human world often appear at the level of many people or firms, rather than the individual. By building up simple processes that reproduce these laws—not an easy task, I might add—researchers have a way to test their understanding in the same way as physics.

Equally important, however, is that these power law patterns offer an aid in getting to grips with systems that simply never seem to settle down, that are always churning and changing and evolving, where nothing seems constant, and nothing is ever quite repeated. Virtually all of past and current social science is based on the notion of equilibrium—on the notion that the various social forces fight with one another and that reality reflects their ultimate balance. Some social scientists have even supposed

that anything that happens in the social world must, by definition, reflect some equilibrium. But what we have seen in this
chapter suggests a very different perspective. Much of the world
is not in equilibrium, but generally very much out of it, perpetually evolving as feedback drives the growth of new patterns that
replace the old, only to be replaced again in the future. People
make fortunes and lose them, sometimes several times in one lifetime. Firms come and go every year. But behind the complexity,
behind the scenes of the outer story, simple mathematical laws
still emerge that reflect the workings of some orderly process.
The human world is no less subject to laws of mathematical precision than the physical.

Chapter 9

FORWARD TO THE PAST

It is all over for priests and gods when man becomes scientific. Moral: science is the forbidden as such—it alone is forbidden. Science is the first sin, seed of all sin, the original sin.

—NIETZSCHE

IN 1968, CONCERNED officials in the state of Vermont attempted to protect the beautiful views of woodland and pasture along its highways, then being spoiled by the signs and unsightly billboards of restaurants and other businesses. State lawmakers had a simple solution—a law banning all billboards and signs over a certain size. In a sense, it worked, as the roads soon had fewer and smaller signs, and yet something else happened too—the spontaneous growth of weird and enormous sculptures. To draw attention to his business, one auto dealer erected a twelve-foot, sixteen-ton gorilla clutching a real Volkswagen Beetle. Not to be outdone, the owner of a carpet store built a huge ceramic teapot with steam and an enormous genie emerging from it, a roll of carpet under his arm. Because these structures weren't displaying messages of any kind, the law didn't apply. The legislature hadn't fully appreciated a notorious principle of the social world—the law of unintended consequences.[1]

Sociologist Robert Merton once wrote a paper on this law entitled "The Unanticipated Consequences of Purposive Social Action."[2] Merton argued that policies designed to achieve certain ends often lead to unexpected outcomes for several reasons. Short-term benefits sometimes seduce us to blank out less desirable longer-term consequences—we enjoy lower taxes today and end up with worse roads and schools in the future. But usually it is simply ignorance and error—the sheer complexity of the social world makes it almost impossible to really foresee the consequences of any one step.

In the late 1970s, U.S. politicians, backed by many economists, concluded that deregulating the airline industry would lead to cheaper fares and better service, by spurring competition between the carriers. Naïvely, this is how the free market is supposed to work, yet it hasn't quite worked out that way. Thirty years later, as transportation writer Alex Marshall observes, we now have "fewer direct flights, fewer airlines, less predictable prices, costly restrictions—and, not incidentally, the financial ruin of nearly every major carrier. Analysts estimate that the airlines have collectively lost more than $50 billion since deregulation began. True, consumers have gotten lower prices on some flights, but only at the cost of astronomical prices on others and a rash of new restrictions and conditions."

What the champions of deregulation failed to appreciate, it seems, is that one of the best ways to compete is to drive your competitors out of business. In the twenty-seven years before 1978, no airline went bankrupt. Since then, 160 have gone bust, and a single major airline now dominates the airports of most large cities; in several of the largest airports, one airline controls more than 90 percent of the originating flights. And as anyone who travels frequently knows, flying has in general become less comfortable as airlines pack ever more customers into smaller spaces. As Marshall points out, the change has also had other unintended consequences:

> Under regulation, the big airlines regularly bought newer and more fuel-efficient airplanes, which translated into lower ticket prices for passengers. But under deregulation, financially troubled airlines could seldom risk spending billions for new planes that would be delivered years later. That's why many planes in the sky today are dangerously old. I suspect that's also why Boeing has declined as a company in recent decades, while the European conglomerate Airbus has thrived. Before deregulation, U.S. airlines bought a new fleet of Boeing planes every few years—which gave Boeing the freedom to innovate and compete commercially.[3]

Of course, you should expect unintended consequences any time you fiddle with a complex system you don't really understand. This has been the fate of mankind in trying to manage the social and economic world through all history. But who says we have to remain ignorant and subject to unintended consequences? We now have a chance to do better.

When the State of Illinois recently decided to deregulate its electricity market, its leaders had the intellectual honesty to recognize that ideology is not equivalent to understanding. Determined not to repeat California's error—in which deregulation enabled Enron and other energy traders to manipulate the market and cheat the public out of billions during the fake power "shortage" of 2000—Illinois enlisted scientists at Argonne National

Laboratory to see if it might run into similar problems. How do you see into the future? It is not so hard, but it takes work and attention to detail. Charles Macal led a team in building a computer model with "agents" to represent individual consumers and regulators, as well as the companies that generate, consume, transmit, and distribute electrical power. The agents explored various strategies for carrying out their business, whatever it might be, and through experience learned and adapted, constantly searching for new strategies that might perform better. Some agents weren't above trying to cheat the market, and Macal's team found that they could: some companies were able to engineer geographical "pockets" in which they could set prices as they wished, an outcome that deregulation is supposed to avoid. Bad news, in one sense, but the team has also found ways to plug the gaps and eliminate the problem. Illinois is still going forward with deregulation, sometime in 2007, but is now doing so with real understanding.

This way of building up insight and knowledge reflects everything I've been writing about in this book. Get a rough picture of the social atom, and of how people interact, then use anything you have, mathematics, the computer, whatever, to learn the kinds of patterns likely to emerge and what their consequences might be. Outside of the social world, this is how all science works. And it is ironic that this is still not the way most social science works. Because this is precisely what the great social thinkers of the past once had in mind.

A MORE NATURAL TRADITION

It is safe to say the economists' traditional idea—that we're all hyperrational calculating machines who unfailingly act in our own self-interest—has not been among the more productive ideas of science. One might even say that it stands out as a monument to the incursion of a completely nonscientific way of thinking into human science—a science that, long ago, had a far more sensible foundation. The Scottish philosopher David Hume, living in the century following Isaac Newton, was a full-blown enthusiast for scientific progress and aimed to understand man as Newton had understood physics—not with pure reason, but with experiment and observation. In *A Treatise on Human Nature,* Hume expressed hope that the "experimental method of reasoning" could help to establish "a science of human nature." Historically, philosophers had viewed man either as a slave to his passions, or as a self-controlled demigod inspired by logic and reason. But observation, Hume argued, tells us that neither view is sufficient. We are at times reasonable creatures, but reason is not often the ruling force: "Men do not normally reason with one another, men impact on one another as billiard balls do; it is custom that leads men to do things as they do; it is custom, often concealed from the actor, which drives him to do things of which he is naturally ignorant as to why and for what purpose he does them."[4]

Writing before Charles Darwin, Hume used "custom" in the broadest sense—referring to social norms, habits, and traditions of behavior, passed down to men either by biology or culture, that constrain and channel the actions of men and make them often do similar things. Among other things, Hume also rejected those who emphasized human greed as the preeminent factor in motivating men and instead saw human altruism as a real element in human character. The idea of man as a selfish creature, he felt, was "contrary to both common feeling and our most unprejudiced notions."

It is no accident, perhaps, that our practical understanding of the social world made roaring progress in Hume's time, largely from the effort of his friend and fellow Scotsman Adam Smith. Like Hume, Smith also had little time for the view that men always act selfishly. Though he is today often described as the original champion of rugged individualism, he believed that a healthy social order could only be achieved when "we feel much for others and little for ourselves." But while Hume focused on capturing the character of the social atom, Smith sought more to perceive how such atoms lead, through interaction, to social outcomes, and often surprises. Smith's book *The Wealth of Nations* has accurately been called "an encyclopedia of the effects of unintended consequences in human affairs."[5] Most famously, of course, Smith argued that individuals, if left to pursue their own ends, will tend to benefit society, even without their intending it. More generally, his overriding concern was to learn how to anticipate the unexpected in social life through sound understanding. Men were typically ruled, Smith believed, more by their passions than by their reasoning faculties, and social improvement could best be achieved by understanding how to "channel" the passions to produce good outcomes.

If both Hume and Smith were alive today, I suspect they would both argue that the level of inequality in wealth—it has dramatically risen in virtually all nations over the past twenty-five years—presents a serious challenge to social cohesion.[6] Smith certainly believed that social patterns created out of individual human activity act back on individuals, altering their behavior. I doubt he would be surprised by modern psychological research demonstrating that people tend to judge their well-being in relative rather than absolute terms, and to judge their wealth by comparing it to that of others around them. In this sense, high levels of inequality will tend to erode human satisfaction. Smith might also point out that today, as in his own time, inequality tends to lead to unproductive "rent-seeking" behavior, as the wealthy take advantage of their power to stifle competition and to extract income from the less wealthy. He would be concerned by trends toward greater inequality for many of the reasons cited in a recent United Nations study, which concluded:

> The divisiveness that comes out of large disparities in income and wealth, is actually reflected in poorer economic performance of a country. Typically when countries are more equal, educational achievement and benefits are more equally distributed in the country. If you have a society with large concentrations of poor families, average school achievement is usually a lot lower than where you have a much more homogenous middle class population, as you find in most Western European countries. So the high level of inequality results in less human capital being developed in this country, which ultimately affects economic performance.[7]

There is no question that Hume and Smith would view the modern idea that individuals are isolated and independent and unaffected by the social world around them as insidious and false. Social patterns feed back to affect individuals and channel their behavior, possibly in destructive ways, but possibly in productive ways, if we can learn how to manage them effectively. What Hume, Smith, and other Enlightenment thinkers didn't realize, and couldn't possibly have realized, is the sheer combinatorial difficulty of doing so, of reckoning with social complexity. While hoping to build a science of the human world in the spirit of physics, they were limited by their tools. Most important, they didn't have the ideas of two centuries of physics to draw on and had no computers to help them examine the consequences of simple rules in an "experimental" way.

Finally, after two centuries, we have the ability to go back and pick up where Hume and Smith left off. We've seen a number of specific examples in earlier chapters. In a more expansive way, perhaps, we may also begin to glimpse some meaningful patterns in human history as a whole.

THE END OF EMPIRE

Karl Marx thought he saw a steady progression in history leading at the far end to world government by the workers. The British historian Arnold Toynbee claimed to see cyclic patterns in the rise and fall of civilizations. Most historians today think that Marx and Toynbee were deluded, and that the pursuit of historical laws is a fool's chase, but it would indeed be weird if the dynamics of every population on earth followed discernible patterns of evolution and change, while we humans somehow escaped the natural logic of form and process. We're probably miles away from understanding the laws of history in any detailed way, but it is amusing—and possibly illuminating as well—to see how we might put together some things we've learned in a guess.

Aside from our individual intelligence, what really sets us apart from other species is our ability to cooperate, even with genetically unrelated strangers. This is perhaps the single most important factor behind our dominance of this planet. "The destruction of the natural world," as John Gray has written, "is not the result of global capitalism, industrialization, 'Western civilization,' or any flaw in human institutions. It is a consequence of the evolutionary success of an exceptionally rapacious primate."[8] And what makes us especially rapacious is our ability to cooperate and coordinate to do what none of us could ever achieve alone.

Our behavioral trait of "strong reciprocity" seems to have had a key bearing on the engineering of our cooperative societies. And one of the most plausible explanations of this trait is that it was created in the forge of a long history of competition and conflict between groups, with the more cooperative surviving. Peter Turchin, professor of ecology and evolutionary biology at the University of Connecticut, has argued in detail that this competition has in fact not ended. Rather, it underlies a natural explanation of the rise and fall of empires through history.[9] This explanation is highly speculative, but illustrates the potential power of combining insights from psychology with an understanding of the logic of patterns and feedback, and, in doing so, to go beyond the usual storytelling mode of historical explanation.

On the world stage, Turchin suggests, ethnic groups—identified by race, language, and other markers—have always competed for resources, land, and so on. Those able to sustain a higher level of group cooperation have tended to prevail, doing a better job of providing a collective defense or in coordinating attacks against others. Russia rose up out of a three-century battle to survive in the face of murderous raids by Tatar bands from the steppes to the south. America grew strong and cohesive during a similarly murderous three-century battle to survive and expand against indigenous peoples. Suggestively, and in rough terms, this is the same explanation applied to cultures that Axtell found to explain the differing abilities of modern business firms to compete and survive.

But this idea, that history is an evolutionary competition between more or less cooperative groups, trails another question in its wake. What happens later to these cooperative groups that undermines their success and would explain why all empires have eventually fallen? It is of course true that the detailed story will in every case be different. The particular constellation of enemies facing an empire, its geographical position, its success or failure in devising new technologies—all should play a role. But behind these details, a more fundamental process may be at work, serving to undo and undermine the cooperation on which any empire's success rests.

Pareto's natural law of wealth suggests that any wealthy nation, by mathematics alone, will have a vast divide between a few wealthy and powerful people and a mass of poor ones. The consequences of such an inequality, as we have just seen, include a breakdown of trust and cooperation and effective economic function. This breakdown may be as deep as it is inevitable. As economist Edward Glaeser and colleagues at Harvard University have documented, for example, inequality tends to give both the powerful and the not powerful the incentive to undermine effective governing institutions, to the detriment of the entire society:

> Inequality can encourage institutional subversion in two distinct ways. First, the have-nots can redistribute from the haves through violence, the political process, or other means. Such "Robin Hood" redistribution jeopardizes property rights, and deters investment by the rich . . . Second, the haves can redistribute from the have-nots by subverting legal, political and regulatory institutions to work in their favor. They can do so through political contributions, bribes, or just deployments of legal and political resources to get their way. This "King John" redistribution renders the property rights of those less well positioned—including small entrepreneurs—insecure, and holds back their investment.[10]

In this view, it could be the very success of an empire that sets up the conditions for its demise, through, in Turchin's words, the "corrosive effect that glaring inequality has on the willingness of people to cooperate."

Although the consequences of inequality offer important warnings, this theory is most interesting because it is more than the usual history, more than a story with facts and dates and decisions. It attempts to explain history by taking account of the fundamental processes that we know must play a role and brings modern science to bear from many points—from psychology and experimental economics to physics. It's likely that there aren't any obvious trends or simple cycles in history; nothing that can be wrapped up in a few equations à la Isaac Newton. But if there is some discernible process to history, with its own characteristic rhythms and features, this is how we will find it—by thinking of patterns, as well as people.

ORGANIZATION IS EVERYTHING

At the beginning of this book, I talked a lot about patterns rather than people; about the notion that a fundamental error in thinking accounts for much of our puzzlement over the human world. We like to find causes in the characters of individual people, as great leaders or evil madmen, for example, and often fail to see that ordinary people acting in ordinary ways can lead to outcomes we would never imagine. We've seen how communities can segregate themselves along racial lines even without racism, and how birthrates in civilized nations can plummet because people begin imitating their neighbors and friends, as if they were buying fashionable shoes. We explored the weird origins of warmhearted human altruism in the cold and brutal history of group competition and combat, and we have seen that this ancient history appears to mirror the growth and dissolution of modern businesses, as cooperation comes and goes. We've seen how this same process might have a lot to do with the rise and fall of empires, which we can think of as businesses writ large on the world stage. And we've seen, in some cases, how a simple logical process, working behind the scenes, can give rise to mathematical laws of the same kind we know from physics, even though individuals continue to have free will and can act as they please.

Insight into these patterns and laws, as we've learned, comes not by celebrating man as some kind of mythical and hyperrational god, but by accepting our place in nature. We imitate one another for the same reason penguins do—to learn valuable information from others with different experience from our own. Modern psychology suggests that our intelligence arises not from accurate calculation, but more than anything else from our ability to learn and adapt. This is, almost always, how we manage to solve problems on our own. More important yet are our skills for solving problems together—by learning to cooperate, or just by one person learning a "good trick" from another. Most important is our ability to manage the interactions that support social cohesion and build the complex webs of relations that make our groups far more than the sum of their parts. We live in an incredibly rich social world, but we shouldn't credit this richness to the richness of any one person—it is the combination of people and their ideas, the actions and reactions, that matters most.

In understanding the social world, the key problem lies in understanding the origin and emergence of social pattern and organization. In this regard, it is no accident that social science now has an increasing resonance with physics. Physicists long ago came into possession of a pretty good picture of the atoms that make up our world and their properties. Today they are engaged in the long project of understanding all the different patterns and kinds of organization those atoms can explore and that lead to the endless forms in the world around us—to substances of all kinds, from snowflakes and leaves to stars, galaxies, and black holes. The more we learn about the importance of organization and form, the more we see it everywhere—even in the most fundamental laws of nature themselves. In the words of Nobel Prize–winning physicist Robert Laughlin:

> I am increasingly persuaded that all physical law that we know about has collective origins, not just some of it. In other words, the distinction between fundamental laws and the laws descending from them is a myth . . . Physical law cannot generally be anticipated by pure thought, but must be discovered experimentally, because control of nature is achieved only when nature allows this through a principle of organization . . . What physical science has to tell us is that the whole being more than the sum of its parts is not merely a concept but a physical phenomenon. Nature is regulated not only by a microscopic rule base, but by powerful and general principles of organization.[11]

In the social world, we are only beginning to glimpse these principles of organization and sense the patterns and hidden forces that make our world what it is. But the discoveries of the past twenty years mark a shift in perspective that will have immense long-term repercussions. Increasingly, we understand the basic forces of organization behind sudden movements in stock markets, behind racial segregation and ethnic hatred, and we can begin to act on this knowledge, and to act with at least a little foresight.

THE OTHER SIDE OF KNOWLEDGE

I cannot end this brief exploration of the exciting possibilities that flow out of a more natural view of the human situation without recognizing that this view has natural enemies. This way of thinking does not demean or devalue human life, but merely accepts that the mathematics and mechanics of the ordinary world apply to us as much as to anything else. This is what we should have expected all along. Yet many people find the scientific way of explaining things disappointing, irritating—maybe even a little threatening. Explanations based on the investigation of facts and relationships, and of the kinds of processes that might have led to those facts, won't sit well with anyone who demands that human life is somehow distinct and separate from the rest of biology. It certainly won't appeal to any of the countless millions who see in world history the revealed miracles of a divine Creator, and for whom the facts of science can only seem like aggressive intrusions upon divine freedom.

This latter category still represents most of the world. When it comes to religion, in the words of philosopher Sam Harris of Stanford University, this is the situation we face:

Most of the people in this world believe that the Creator of the Universe has written a book. We have the misfortune of having many such books on hand, each making an exclusive claim as to its infallibility . . . Each of these texts urges its readers to adopt a variety of beliefs and practices, some of which are benign, many of which are not. All are in perverse agreement on one point of fundamental importance, however: "respect" for other faiths, or for the views of unbelievers, is not an attitude that God endorses.[12]

It seems all too likely that religions exist for a reason; like ethnocentric prejudice, religious faith has, through the energies and devotion it inspires, paid dividends in the past, to our ancestors and the groups to whom they belonged. Many of our brains are, I suspect, "prepared" to be religious in much the same way they are prepared to make instinctive decisions, about whom to trust, for example. Blind faith is perhaps the ultimate weapon of group unity. If we were all one group, this would be okay. We could live our lives as if in a cosmic dream, believing what we like, and getting along with one another. But religious groups, convinced of their righteousness, have slaughtered one another, and nonbelievers, through history. It is hard to believe the future won't see more of the same, only with vastly more powerful weapons. In this regard, our persisting instincts for religion may be our most dangerous "maladaptation."

In fact, it is the philosophical spillover from religious thinking that ultimately lies behind the long-enthroned vision of man as a perfectly rational creature, set on a pedestal above the rest of nature. The same roots feed the notion that social science, in its essence, must be different from physical science; that we must carve a sharp dividing line through the world, with humanity on one side, nature on the other. But we are a part of nature, and we shall only understand ourselves better if we learn to accept this. If we do, we have a better chance to go "forward to the past," picking up the torch from Hume, Smith, and their contemporaries, and approaching the world with optimism and confidence that we can find the truth, whatever it may be. We're sure to be confused for many years, perhaps always. But we can at least embrace the laudable view expressed by the German playwright Gotthold Lessing in 1778:

> Not the truth in whose possession any man is, or thinks he is, but the honest effort he has made to find out the truth, is what constitutes the worth of a man. For it is not through the possession but the inquiry after truth that his powers expand, and in this alone consists his ever-growing perfection.

ACKNOWLEDGMENTS

Many people have helped me in the writing of this book. I must thank the many researchers whose inspiring work and ideas I have drawn upon, and I encourage readers to track down the original references and read them, for they are invariably richer than my short accounts would suggest. Kerry Nugent Wells of the Garamond Agency, and her colleagues Lisa Adams and David Miller, deserve immense credit for helping me to form the basic ideas and argument of the book; it would have been far more confusing and unfocused without their efforts. Finally, as always, my wife, Kate, not only tolerated my difficult and inexplicable mood swings over many months of writing and inspired me to keep going, but read the entire book over many (far too many) times, correcting numerous errors and improving the presentation everywhere.

NOTES

PREFACE

1. Schelling's famous paper on segregation appeared in the very first issue of the *Journal of Mathematical Sociology*. The reference is T. C. Schelling, *Journal of Mathematical Sociology* 1 (1971): 143–86. It should, of course, go without saying that the model does not prove that real-world segregation has nothing to do with racist attitudes. Racism may indeed be a factor. However, the model establishes that one cannot infer the influence of racism merely from the presence of persisting segregation. It proves, most dramatically, that other, hidden processes may be at work, and that any real science of segregation had better come to terms with them. Schelling explored this way of thinking more extensively in a later book, *Micromotives and Macrobehavior* (London and New York: W. W. Norton, 1978).

2. Ironically, while I was partially through writing this book, Schelling was awarded the 2005 Nobel Prize in economics. For some background on his way of thinking—which has long been at odds with most mainstream economics— I highly recommend his Nobel Prize address. The video is available at http://nobelprize.org/nobel_prizes/economics/

laureates/2005/schelling-lecture.html. The text is available at http://nobelprize.org/nobel_prizes/economics/laureates/2005/schelling-lecture.pdf.

Chapter 1: THINK PATTERNS, NOT PEOPLE

1. Peter Maass, *Love Thy Neighbor* (New York: Knopf, 1996).
2. Sebastian Haffner, *Defying Hitler* (London: Weidenfeld & Nicolson, 2003).
3. A fascinating interview with Philip Zimbardo is available online at http://www.edge.org/3rd_culture/zimbardo05/zimbardo05_index.html.
4. M. A. Kessler and B. T. Werner, "Self-Organization of Sorted Patterned Ground," *Science* 299 (2003): 380–83.
5. The original paper is D. Helbing, I. Farkas, and T. Vicsek, *Physical Review Letters* 84 (2000): 1240–43. You can view lanes forming in simulations at Dirk Helbing's Web site. See http://rcswww.urz.tu-dresden.de/~helbing/Pedestrians/Corridor.html.
6. The original paper is D. Helbing, I. Farkas, and T. Vicsek, *Nature* 407 (2000): 487–90. You can view a simulation of the escape scenario, and how a properly positioned table can help, at http://angel.elte.hu/~panic/.
7. Here, for example, is Craig Calhoun, former editor of the journal *Sociological Theory,* talking about the kinds of papers he typically received for publication—certainly far more respectable than their postmodern cousins—but still lacking a certain spirit of adventure. They were, Calhoun recalls, "summaries of what dead people said, with no indication of why living ones should care or how the revered ancestor's work would advance contemporary analytic projects." Or,

worse: "criticisms of what other people have said that dead people said, with no more indication of why we should care than that those criticized are famous."

For further discussion of these attitudes and related points, see Peter Hedström, *Dissecting the Social* (New York: Cambridge University Press, 2005). Clearly, this isn't a particularly encouraging sign for any area of science, where the past is supposed to provide a springboard to a better future. As the British philosopher Alfred North Whitehead once put it, "A science which hesitates to forget its founders is lost."

8. Strangeness isn't a foolproof sign of intellectual claptrap, but a determined unwillingness to express ideas clearly usually is. Here's a typical example of postmodernist clarity from the work of a famous theorist, Félix Guattari:

> We can clearly see that there is no bi-univocal correspondence between linear signifying links or archi-writing, depending on the author, and this multireferential, multidimensional machinic catalysis. The symmetry of scale, the transversality, the pathic nondiscursive character of their expansion: all these dimensions remove us from the logic of the excluded middle and reinforce us in our dismissal of the ontological binarism we criticised previously.

In 1996, suspecting that postmodern theory might not be endowed with the deep meaning it pretends to be, physicist Alan Sokol performed a test. He wrote a paper of complete nonsense entitled "Transgressing the Boundaries: Towards a Transformative Hermeneutics of Quantum Gravity." The sentences of the text played by the rules of grammar, and Sokol threw in lots of postmodern buzzwords such as *hermeneutic, deconstruct,* and so forth, but the article was otherwise entirely devoid of meaning. Sokol then submitted the manuscript to the prominent postmodernist journal *Social Text*, where it was duly reviewed, accepted, and published. For another amusing demonstration of how easy it is to generate apparently "deep" writing in the postmodern style, visit the Postmodernism Generator (http://www.elsewhere.org/pomo), where a computer program written by Andrew Bulhak will automatically write you an impressive manuscript. The article it just wrote for me in less than a second, "Neotextual Theory in the Works of Spelling," begins:

> "Society is intrinsically a legal fiction," says Foucault; however, according to von Ludwig,[1] it is not so much society that is intrinsically a legal fiction, but rather the stasis of society. De Selby[2] implies that we have to choose between dialectic deconstruction and dialectic objectivism. It could be said that Lacan's analysis of neotextual theory holds that academe is capable of intention, but only if narrativity is equal to reality.

Chapter 2: The "Human" Problem

1. William Stern, "The Unexpected Lessons of Times Square's Comeback," *City Journal*, Autumn 1999. See http://www.city-journal.org/html/9_4_the_unexpected.html.
2. Pierre Gassendi, *Tycho Brahe: The Man and His Work* (original in Latin) (1654).
3. For an animation that shows clearly how things work, see the NASA Web site http://mars.jpl.nasa.gov/allabout/nightsky/nightsky04-2003animation.html. In principle, if the orbits of Mars and Earth were in precisely the same plane, Mars's mo-

tion would remain on a single curve across the sky, rather than forming a loop. The precise details of the retrograde trajectory reflect further complexity of planetary motion, in particular the fact that the two planets' orbits lie in slightly different planes.

4. Some of the most accurate calculations in this area come from Toichiro Kinoshita of Cornell University. His colleague at Cornell Jim Sethna offers a nice description at http://www.lassp.cornell.edu/sethna/Cracks/QED.html.

5. I say "largely" because, as I noted in chapter 1, many social researchers do look for statistical correlations between social variables, which is roughly akin to Kepler's search for patterns in planetary motion. But the kinds of correlations discovered typically lack the universal character as well as the simplicity of Kepler's patterns. More important, however, social researchers have traditionally failed to follow up the discovery of correlations with convincing explanations based on simple mechanisms. It is hard to find any example in social research of the recipe for good science as illustrated by Brahe, Kepler, and Newton.

6. Henry Thomas Buckle, *History of Civilization in England* (London: 1857), 1: 6–7.

7. John Kay, "Cracks in the Crystal Ball," *Financial Times,* September 29, 1995.

8. Friedrich Nietzsche, *Beyond Good and Evil* (New York: Random House, 1992), 202.

9. Edward Hallett Carr, *What Is History?* (New York: Penguin, 1990), 14.

10. This view seems fairly ludicrous to me and, fortunately, isn't taken too seriously by researchers really trying to understand social forces.

11. Fyodor Dostoyevsky, *Notes from Underground* (New York: Dover Books, 1992).

12. Karl Popper, *The Poverty of Historicism* (London: ARK Publishing, 1957).

Chapter 3: OUR THINKING INSTINCTS

1. Isaiah Berlin, *Concepts and Categories* (New York: Pimlico, 1999), 159.

2. This explanation was proposed two years ago by mathematician Steve Strogatz of Cornell University and colleagues (*Nature* 438 [2005]: 43–44), who found that the basic aspects of the event can be explained with equations that physicists use to describe the collective oscillations of millions of tiny electrical devices or crickets synchronizing their chirping in a field, all through feedback and self-organization. The full story, however, may not be quite so simple. Although there is little doubt that some kind of feedback between the people and the bridge caused the oscillation, there are, in Strogatz's words, "many lingering mysteries about how pedestrians interact with wobbly bridges." The City of London has since installed huge brakes on the bridge that keep it stable.

3. The classic popular exposition of the ideas of chaos still remains James Gleick's *Chaos* (New York: Penguin, 1987).

4. Francis Galton, *The Art of Travel* (London: Weidenfeld & Nicolson, 2000).

5. Gary Becker, Nobel Prize lecture, 1992. This lecture is available online at http://home.uchicago.edu/~gbecker/Nobel/nobellecture.pdf.

6. D. K. Foley, "Introduction," in *Barriers and Bounds to Rational-*

ity, ed. P. S. Albin (Princeton: Princeton University Press, 1998), 3–72.

7. Modern economic theory, and its near reverence for rationality, has come in for withering criticism from many thinkers both inside and outside the profession. Among many other books, Richard Thaler's *Winner's Curse* (Princeton: Princeton University Press, 1992) offers a wealth of empirical evidence regarding ordinary people and their systematic deviations from the rational ideal. Paul Ormerod's *Death of Economics* (London: Faber and Faber, 1994) offers an impassioned critique of the whole of traditional economics. Robert Solow's essay "How Did Economics Get That Way and What Way Did It Get?" in *American Academic Culture in Transformation* (Princeton: Princeton University Press, 1997) is more upbeat; he rightly, in my view, celebrates the economic practice of building simple models of real-world processes, while also deploring the excessive fascination with perfect individual rationality. Perhaps the most fascinating and damning critique of the peculiar character of modern economic theory is Robert Nelson's *Economics as Religion* (University Park: Pennsylvania State University Press, 2001). Nelson argues that the assumption of rationality, and much of the ostentatious mathematical formalism of modern economics, actually finds its roots in the ideological struggle of the Cold War, and the necessity to counter the supposed "science" of Marxism with a supposed "science" that would prove the superiority of the free market. This was achieved most readily, he argues, with a formalism that suggested mathematical certainty. There are literally thousands of articles arguing over the pros and cons of looking at people as rational actors. Today, however, this

debate looks increasingly sterile, as other, more effective ways of doing social science are pushing this perspective into the history books. For a provocative view on where economic theory is heading as it becomes more realistic, see Richard Thaler, "From Homo Economicus to Homo Sapiens," *Journal of Economic Perspectives* 14 (2000): 133–41.

8. Robert Axelrod, "Advancing the art of simulation in the social sciences," in *Simulating Social Phenomena*, ed. Rosaria Conte, Rainer Hegselmann, and Pietro Terna (Berlin: Springer, 1997), 21–40. Axelrod may have come to this conclusion in part from an amusing experience he had as a student in an economics lecture. As he recalls, "I distinctly remember an occasion when a professor—a future Nobel Prize winner—was presenting a formal model of consumer behavior. A student remarked, 'But that's not how people behave.' The professor replied simply, 'You're right,' and without another word, turned back to the blackboard and continued with his presentation of the model. We all got the point."

9. Thaler, "From Homo Economicus."

10. You will find a nice discussion of how irrational investors can beat the rational ones in Andrei Shleifer, *Inefficient Markets* (Oxford: Oxford University Press, 2000).

11. A very readable introduction to Kahneman's work and that of others in this area is Daniel Kahneman, Nobel Prize lecture, 2002. This is available online at http://nobelprize.org/nobel_prizes/economics/laureates/2002/kahneman-lecture.html.

12. Gigerenzer's book offers a fascinating discussion of many similar puzzles that defeat our thinking minds. Gerd Gigerenzer, *Reckoning with Risk* (London: Penguin, 2002).

13. This nice phrase appears in the clear and concise *Evolutionary*

Psychology: A Primer, by Leda Cosmides and John Tooby. This can be found online at http://www.psych.ucsb.edu/research/cep/primer.html.

14. M. K. Chen, V. Lakshminarayanan, and L. Santos, *Journal of Political Economy*, forthcoming. A draft is available online at http://www.som.yale.edu/Faculty/keith.chen/papers/LossAversionDraft.pdf. For more on loss aversion in humans, see Kahneman's Nobel Prize lecture.

15. Benjamin Libet, *Behavioural and Brain Sciences* 8 (1985).

16. Francis Fukayama, *Trust* (New York: Simon and Schuster, 1995).

Chapter 4: THE ADAPTIVE ATOM

1. Brian Arthur, "Inductive Reasoning and Bounded Rationality," *American Economic Review* 84, no. 2 (Papers and Proceedings of the Hundred and Sixth Annual Meeting of the American Economic Association) (May 1994): 406–11.

2. A nice introduction to the mathematics of derivative pricing is Paul Wilmott, Sam Howison, and Jeff Dewynne, *The Mathematics of Financial Derivatives* (Cambridge: Cambridge University Press, 1995). One of the elegant and surprising aspects of this area is a deep link to the mathematical physics of heat flow; equations of essentially the same character come into play in either case. The Nobel Prize lectures of Merton and Scholes can be found at http://nobelprize.org/nobel_prizes/economics/laureates/1997/press.html.

3. The story of Long-Term Capital Management is told in Nicholas Dunbar, *Inventing Money* (Chichester: John Wiley & Sons, 2000).

4. The widespread applicability of the bell curve is the consequence of something that mathematicians call the central limit

theorem. This imposing name refers to a simple fact: In any case in which a huge number of independent influences contribute to the outcome of some event, then that event will fall onto the bell curve. Roll a die a hundred times and add up the numbers. Now do it again, and again, and plot the results. You are guaranteed to find a distribution like the bell curve, centered about an average of 350. This is guaranteed because each of the hundred contributing rolls is independent of the others. The central limit theorem is an extremely powerful bit of mathematics, but that is not to say that everything follows a bell curve. A discovery of modern science is that an equally enormous number of things do not.

5. This conclusion is not obvious from what I have said, but follows from a somewhat more technical argument. The typical argument is that the many factors that influence a stock's price do so independently. If one influence pushes it up, this makes it no more likely that another will push it up rather than down. If many such influences have no relationship or link to one another, then central limit theorem of mathematics implies that the distribution of overall changes should lie on the bell curve.

6. Benoit Mandelbrot, *Journal of Business* 36 (1963): 294.

7. P. Gopikrishnan, M. Meyer, L. A. N. Amaral, and H. E. Stanley, *European Physical Journal B* 3 (1998): 139.

8. R. N. Mantegna, "Levy walks and enhanced diffusion in the Milan stock exchange," *Physica A* 179 (1991): 232.

9. O. V. Pictet et al., "Statistical study of foreign exchange rates, empirical evidence of a price change scaling law and intraday analysis," *Journal of Banking and Finance* 14 (1995): 1189–1208.

10. D. Cutler, J. Poterba, and L. Summers, *Review of Economic Studies* 58 (1991): 529–46.

11. Arthur, "Inductive Reasoning and Bounded Rationality." Available online at http://www.santafe.edu/arthur/Papers/El_Farol.html.

12. It is important to point out that the behavior in Arthur's bar model does not depend sensitively on the number of people, the supposed threshold at which the bar gets crowded, or precisely how people begin to suffer as it does get crowded. It is clearly unrealistic to suppose that people have a wonderful time if forty-nine people show up, but a horrible time if another two walk in to make fifty-one. Arthur used this just as a simplification. Simulations with more realistic assumptions give much the same outcome.

13. Eugene Wigner, *Communications in Pure and Applied Mathematics* 13, no. 1 (1960), http://www.dartmouth.edu/~matc/MathDrama/reading/Wigner.html.

14. W. B. Arthur, J. Holland, B. LeBaron, R. Palmer, and P. Tayler, "Asset pricing under endogenous expectations in an artificial stock market," in *The Economy as an Evolving Complex System II,* ed. W. B. Arthur, S. Durlauf, and D. Lane (Reading, MA: Addison-Wesley, 1997), 15–44.

15. A number of different kinds of models are under development, all of which treat the market as a collection of goal-oriented agents who can learn and adapt to their environment by altering their strategies. This, rather than the older "rational agent" point of view, would seem to be the wave of the future. Representative examples of work in this area include T. Lux and M. Marchesi, *Nature* 397 (1999): 498–500; and D. Challet, A. Chessa, M. Marsili, and Y.-C. Zhang, *Journal of Quantitative Finance* 1 (2001): 168. A recent and up-to-date review is T. Galla, G. Mosetti, and Y.-C. Zhang, "Anomalous fluctuations in

Minority Games and related multi-agent models of financial markets," http://www.arxiv.org/pdf/physics/0608091.

16. Milton Friedman, *Essays in Positive Economics* (Chicago: University of Chicago Press, 1953), 14.

17. When we see someone who has won, most of us seem ready to attribute such success to skill rather than anything else. Even so, it is clear that among all the many mutual funds, one of them must come out on top every year, even if this is due entirely to random luck. Academic studies suggest that the ups and downs of market prices are essentially unpredictable, except for some rare (and usually temporary) exceptions. Studies several years ago, for example, showed that stock values in the recent past had shown a significant tendency to rise in January, a phenomenon which became known as the January Effect. After it became widely known, however, this effect disappeared. It has also been noted that stocks that fall the most in one year are more likely than the average stock to rise in the following year—presumably because investors overreacted and pushed the price down too far to begin with. For a discussion of a number of such oddities, revealing some degree of predictability amid the normal sea of unpredictable chaos, see Andrei Shleifer's *Inefficient Markets* (Oxford: Oxford University Press, 2000).

18. John Kenneth Galbraith, *A History of Economics* (London: Penguin, 1987), 4.

19. See N. Gupta, R. Hauser, and N. F. Johnson, "Using artificial markets to forecast financial time-series," available as a preprint at http://www.arxiv.org/pdf/physics/0506134.

20. I've written about this in "Supermodels to the rescue," *strategy + business* 38 (2004).

21. For more on this fascinating work, see Luc Steels, *The Talking*

Heads Experiment, Volume I, Words and Meanings (Antwerp: Labrotorium, 1999). See also, for example, Andrea Baronchelli et al., "Sharp Transition Towards Shared Vocabularies in Multi-Agent Systems," *Journal of Statistical Mechanics* P06014 (2006).

Chapter 5: THE IMITATING ATOM

1. For a fascinating account of this episode, see Robert Bartholomew and Simon Wessely, "Epidemic hysteria in Virginia," *Southern Medical Journal* 92 (1999): 762–69.
2. The classic on such manias is Charles Mackay's *Extraordinary Popular Delusions and the Madness of Crowds* (New York: Three Rivers Press, 1980), originally published in 1841.
3. The term *embeddedness* has taken a somewhat special place in social theory, following an influential 1985 paper of sociologist Mark Granovetter. Granovetter argued a point that most people would accept, but that ran counter to the received economic wisdom of the time—that the behavior of individuals or firms is affected by the people or other firms with whom they interact. Believe it or not, this was a radical idea. His paper is "Economic Action and Social Structure: The Problem of Embeddedness," *American Journal of Sociology* 91 (1985): 485–510. Granovetter's thinking was inspired by the earlier writing of Karl Polanyi, who had suggested, "The human economy is embedded and enmeshed in institutions, economic and noneconomic. The inclusion of the noneconomic is vital. For religion or government may be as important to the structure and the functioning of the economy as monetary institutions or the availability of tools and machines themselves that lighten the toil of labor." This text is from K. Polanyi, C. Arensberg, and H. Pearson, eds., *Trade and*

Market in the Early Empires: Economies in History and Theory (Chicago: Henry Regnery, 1957).

4. A classic paper on imitation, a joy to read, and a resource for many of the examples cited in this chapter, is S. Bikhchandani, D. Hirshleifer, and I. Welch, "Learning from the behavior of others: conformity, fads and informational cascades," *Journal of Economic Perspectives* 12 (1998): 151–70.

5. Solomon Asch, "Studies of independence and conformity: A minority of one against a unanimous majority," *Psychological Monographs* 70 (1956). A nice description of the experiment can be found online at http://www.age-of-the-sage.org/psychology/social/asch_conformity.html.

6. Solomon Asch, "Opinions and social pressure," *Scientific American* 193 (1955): 33–35. A review of 133 experiments performed since the 1950s, along lines similar to Asch's, suggests that the tendency toward social conformity has grown somewhat weaker over the past fifty years. See Rod Bond and Peter Smith, *Psychological Bulletin* 119 (1996): 111–37.

7. G. S. Burns et al., *Biological Psychiatry* 58 (2005): 245–53.

8. See Christophe Chamley, *Rational Herds* (Cambridge: Cambridge University Press, 2004).

9. Bikhchandani, Hirshleifer, and Welch, "Learning from the behavior," 151–70.

10. See Edward Glaeser, Bruce Sacerdote, and Jose Schienkman, "Crime and Social Interactions," *Quarterly Journal of Economics* 111 (1996): 507–48.

11. Mark Granovetter, "Threshold Models of Collective Behavior," *American Journal of Sociology* 83 (1978): 1420–43.

12. Q. Michard and J.-P. Bouchaud, "Theory of collective opinion shifts: From smooth trends to abrupt swings," *European Physical Journal B* 47 (2005): 151–59.

Chapter 6: THE COOPERATIVE ATOM

1. Thompson's harrowing description of his experiences during the tsunami is available online at http://www.sonomacounty law.com/tsunami/timeline.htm.

2. Joseph Alexander, *Utmost Savagery* (New York: Random House, 1995).

3. This idea, known as kin selection, was originally proposed by the late biologist William Hamilton. The original reference is William Hamilton, "The genetical evolution of social behavior. I, II," *Journal of Theoretical Biology* 7 (1964): 1–16, 17–52. An excellent exposition of this way of thinking is Richard Dawkins, *The Extended Phenotype* (Oxford: Oxford University Press, 1982).

4. Quoted in Frans de Waal, "How Animals Do Business," *Scientific American,* April 2005, 73–79.

5. Robert Frank, *Passions Within Reason: The Strategic Role of the Emotions* (New York: W. W. Norton, 1991).

6. David Hume, *A Treatise of Human Nature*, ed. L. A. Selby-Bigge and P. H. Nidditch (Oxford: Clarendon Press, 1975).

7. The story of the two farmers is a version of the famous Prisoner's Dilemma, an imaginary scenario invented by Merrill Flood and Melvin Dresher in the 1950s to explore the logic of strategic behavior in competitive situations. In their original scenario, the police are interrogating two prisoners held in separate cells. Each can either confess to the crime the two committed together or stay silent. If both remain quiet, they'll each get a short sentence (convicted on a lesser charge). If they both confess, they'll get an intermediate sentence, with time reduced slightly for their cooperation. For the pair, staying silent is clearly the better outcome. But an additional element in the

situation leads to the dilemma. The police offer each prisoner a deal—if you rat on your partner and agree to testify against him, we'll set you free. The partner would then get the maximum sentence, a long time indeed. The prisoners now face a tricky situation. If they can trust each other and stay quiet, they'll get the light sentence. But each has the temptation to cheat, sticking his partner with the maximum sentence while he goes free.

Game theory shows that cheating is the best or "dominant" strategy in such a situation, meaning that a person faced with this situation will do better by cheating than by cooperating (staying quiet) regardless of what the other person does. If the other prisoner confesses, your confession gives you an intermediate sentence, rather than a long one. If he stays quiet, your confession gets you off totally free. As a result, one should expect both (rational) people facing such a situation to cheat (confess), which is of course somewhat unfortunate for them—their failure to cooperate means they get the intermediate sentence, rather than the short sentence. For a fascinating history of the Prisoner's Dilemma and the scientists who first explored its logic, see William Poundstone, *Prisoner's Dilemma* (New York: Random House, 1992). The Prisoner's Dilemma (and related games) played an important role in strategic analyses of the Cold War standoff between the United States and the USSR. Fortunately, politicians did not always take heed of the lessons emerging from the "rational" analyses of these simple games. In the early 1950s, the brilliant mathematician John von Neumann, one of the founders of game theory, famously argued that the only rational course for the United States was to immediately launch a full-blown and unprovoked nuclear attack on the Soviet Union.

8. The idea of reciprocal altruism was first introduced by biologist Robert Trivers in "The evolution of reciprocal altruism," *Quarterly Review of Biology* 46 (1971): 35–57. Today researchers continue to explore the logic of reciprocal altruism, which turns out to be a little subtler than it first appears. It can be explored by thinking about how two parties will behave if they play a Prisoner's Dilemma game not just once, but many times—the "iterated" Prisoner's Dilemma.

In fact, if the players are strictly rational, they won't learn to cooperate, at least not if they meet for a finite number of times. Here's why. Suppose they are to meet one hundred times. A rational player would first think about what would happen on the final meeting. On this meeting, with no future encounters to come, neither player has any incentive to try to elicit cooperative behavior in the future by being nice now. So on the final meeting, both players will reason, the wise move is to cheat. Hence, cheating by both players on the final meeting is a foregone conclusion. What about the ninety-ninth meeting? As the outcome of the one hundredth is now settled, there is now no reason to try to cooperate on the ninety-ninth meeting either. So cheating is the certain outcome there too. And so on. By this logic, two rational players will reason their way back to the beginning and will decide never to cooperate. Unfortunately, this means they also do much worse than two players who didn't think so deeply. Not surprisingly, perhaps, and fortunately, real people don't approach real-world Prisoner's Dilemmas in this way. Early studies in the 1950s found that even in games of a fixed number of meetings, players rapidly learn that they do better by cooperating.

Perhaps the most fascinating study of the logic of reciprocal altruism was undertaken by political scientist Robert Axelrod in the 1980s. Axelrod set up a tournament in which scientists of many different persuasions submitted logical strategies for playing the iterated Prisoner's Dilemma. Each strategy would determine whether the player should cooperate or defect in the next game, based on the behavior of the other player in the recent past. Researchers submitted a number of highly sophisticated algorithms for playing, but one of the simplest strategies actually won the tournament. This strategy is tit for tat: you cooperate in the first game, and then, each round, do precisely what the other player did in the preceding round—you cooperate if the other cooperated, and defect if the other defected. This strategy punishes defection and rewards cooperation. As Axelrod put it, "What accounts for TIT-FOR-TAT's robust success is its combination of being nice, retaliatory, forgiving and clear. Its niceness prevents it from getting into unnecessary trouble. Its retaliation discourages the other side from persisting whenever defection is tried. Its forgiveness helps restore mutual co-operation. And its clarity makes it intelligible to the other player, thereby eliciting long-term co-operation."

Axelrod's classic book on this and other work related to reciprocal altruism is *The Evolution of Cooperation* (New York: Basic Books, 1985).

9. Quoted in Robert Axelrod, *The Evolution of Cooperation* (New York: Basic Books, 1985).

10. Ibid.

11. Ibid.

12. For more on this see Leda Cosmides and John Tooby, *Evolutionary Psychology: A Primer,* available online at http://www.psych.ucsb.edu/research/cep/primer.html.

13. See Joseph Henrich et al., "In Search of Homo Economicus: Behavioral Experiments in 15 Small-Scale Societies," *American Economic Review* 91 (2001): 73–78.

14. Researchers have experimented with a number of these games in recent years, all of which have many fascinating variations. For an overview see Ernst Fehr and Urs Fischbacher, "The Nature of Human Altruism," *Nature* 425 (2003): 785–91.

15. See Robert Frank, Thomas Gilovich, and Dennis Regan, "Does Studying Economics Inhibit Cooperation?" *Journal of Economic Perspectives* 7 (1993): 159–71; and also Robert Frank, Thomas Gilovich, and Dennis Regan, "Do Economists Make Bad Citizens?" *Journal of Economic Perspectives* 10 (1996): 187–92.

16. The study looked at individuals playing the iterated Prisoner's Dilemma. See James Rilling et al., "A neural basis for social cooperation," *Neuron* 35 (2002): 395–405.

17. Dominique J.-F. de Quervain et al., "The Neural Basis of Altruistic Punishment," *Science* 305 (2004): 1254–58.

18. "Accessing Technology Transfer," 1966 NASA report SP-5067, p. 9–10.

19. Terence Burnham and Dominic Johnson, "The Biological and Evolutionary Logic of Human Cooperation," *Analyse & Kritik* 27 (2005): 113–35.

20. Ernst Fehr and Joseph Henrich, "Is Strong Reciprocity a Maladaptation?" in *The Genetic and Cultural Evolution of Cooperation,* ed. P. Hammerstein (Cambridge: MIT Press, 2005).

21. Gareth Hardin, "The Tragedy of the Commons," *Science* 162 (1968): 1243–48. Also available online at http://dieoff.com/page95.htm.

22. See Fehr and Fischbacher, "Nature of Human Altruism," 785–91.

23. Ernst Fehr and Simon Gachter, "Altruistic Punishment in Humans," *Nature* 415 (2002): 137–40.

24. Reay Tannahill, ed., *Paris in the Revolution* (London: The Folio Society, 1966).

25. Robert Wright, *Nonzero* (New York: Pantheon, 2000).

26. Traditional economics suggests that employee performance can be improved by the threat of sanctions. But our sense of fairness leads to some surprises. In experiments, for example, Ernst Fehr and colleagues have found that the use of sanctions can sometimes lead to a decrease in employees' efforts, as they respond to perceived unfair treatment. It is a lesson learned long ago by animal trainers—that rewards work better than sanctions. That's not to say that sanctions are useless. In some cases, it turns out, they can be beneficial—but mostly if they are *not* used. In further experiments, Fehr and colleagues found that employees respond best when sanctions are in principle possible—spelled out in a contract, for example—but management never or rarely uses them. Employees see the nonuse of possible sanctions as a cooperative act and respond out of gratitude with increased effort, greater even than in the absence of any sanctioning possibilities.

Chapter 7: TOGETHER, APART

1. As Power documents in her brilliant but disheartening *A Problem from Hell: America in the Age of Genocide* (New York: Basic Books, 2002), people of all nations, and Americans in particular, have responded to genocidal conflicts throughout the past century with characteristic disbelief and inaction. Faced with overwhelming evidence from credible witnesses, with photos and films documenting atrocities, with bodies

piled in mass graves, the vast majority of politicians, journalists, and ordinary citizens have always been slow to respond—as if somehow it seems almost impossible to believe.

2. Friedrich von Hayek, *The Road to Serfdom* (London: Routledge, 1944).

3. Sherif's classic study is available online at http://psychclassics .yorku.ca/Sherif/.

4. See "Pardons Granted 88 Years After Crimes of Sedition," *New York Times*, May 3, 2006.

5. There could be other, more complicated strategies, of course. For example, a yellow might decide to cooperate with greens and blues, but not with reds or other yellows. We will ignore these to keep the model simple. Including such strategies, it turns out, has only a minor effect on the results.

6. In their computer study, Axelrod and Hammond did not actually include learning, but instead supposed that those who do well (prosper in their interactions with others) tend to have more offspring than those who do not. This leads to the numerical spreading of people having the same traits, both color and strategy. As they note, however, this dynamic is similar to having a fixed number of people in the population and letting individuals learn to copy the strategies of those who are doing well. Both provide a mechanism for effective strategies to displace ineffective strategies.

7. Ross Hammond and Robert Axelrod, "The Evolution of Ethnocentrism," available online at http://www-personal.umich .edu/~axe/research/Hammond-Ax_Ethno.pdf.

8. Peter J. Richerson and Robert Boyd, *Not By Genes Alone: How Culture Transformed Human Evolution* (Chicago: University of Chicago Press, 2004). See also Richard McElreath, Robert Boyd, and Peter J. Richerson, "Shared norms and the

evolution of ethnic markers," *Current Anthropology* 44 (2003): 122–29.

9. Power, *Problem from Hell.*

10. While the force from a single atom is minuscule, the combined force of all the atoms in a small piece of iron (the number of roughly 1 followed by twenty-four zeros) is appreciable.

Chapter 8: CONSPIRACIES AND NUMBERS

1. Paul Fussell mentions this example in his brilliant book *Wartime* (Oxford: Oxford University Press, 1989), which explores the role of rumors and other psychological devices in helping to assuage the natural fears and uncertainties of soldiers and civilians in times of war.

2. Donna Kossy, *Kooks: A Guide to the Outer Limits of Human Belief* (Los Angeles: Feral House, 1994).

3. See, for example, Edward Wolff, "Changes in Household Wealth in the 1980s and 1990s in the U.S.," Working Paper No. 407, The Levy Economics Institute. Available online at www.levy.org.

4. Donald Brown, "Human Universals, Human Nature and Human Culture," *Daedalus* 33 (2004): 47–54.

5. J. Flemming and J. Micklewright, "Income Distribution, Economic Systems and Transition," Innocenti Occasional Papers, Economic and Social Policy Series No. 70 (Florence: UNICEF International Child Development Centre, 1999). Also see Michael Alexeev, "The Effect of Privatization on Wealth Distribution in Russia," Working Paper No. 86 (The William Davidson Institute, 1998).

6. John Kenneth Galbraith, *A History of Economics* (London: Penguin, 1991).

7. Many economic models along standard lines have been proposed in an attempt to explain the distribution of wealth.
They generally involve appeals to many complex factors working together. For example, one paper on the topic suggests
that issues such as "changes in earnings, including business
ownership, higher rates of return on high asset levels, random
capital gains, government programs to guarantee a minimum
level of consumption, and changes in health and marital status" should all enter into an adequate description, despite the
universality of the data across countries. See V. Quadrini and
J. V. Rios-Rull, "Understanding the U.S. Distribution of
Wealth," *Federal Reserve Bank of Minneapolis Quarterly Review*
21 (1997): 22–36.

8. Jean-Philippe Bouchaud and Marc Mezard, "Wealth condensa-
tion in a simple model of economy," *Physica A* 282 (2000): 536.

9. To be clear, this doesn't mean that intelligence and hard work
don't count for anything, only that luck seems to be the
dominant factor. In fact, economists have long suspected that
luck plays an important role. For example, Harvard professor
Christopher Jencks and colleagues long ago argued that income inequality among genetically related brothers, raised in
similar environments, is roughly as great as for the population
as a whole. See Christopher Jencks, *Inequality* (New York: Basic Books, 1972).

10. See M. Simkin and V. Roychowdhury, "Theory of aces: high
score by skill or luck?" available online at http://www.arxiv
.org/pdf/physics/0607109. The physicist Enrico Fermi made
a similar point to U.S. general Leslie Groves during the Man-
hattan Project to make the first atomic bomb. Fermi asked
Groves for his definition of a "great general," and Groves said
it was someone who wins five battles in a row. "How many

great generals are there?" Fermi then asked, to which Groves replied with an estimate of about three in every one hundred. Fermi pointed out that if generals win completely by luck, then the chance of winning five battles in a row should be one in thirty-two. So, out of one hundred generals, you should find that about three win five in a row. Great generals, Fermi concluded, are made by luck rather than skill.

11. Other researchers have now taken this initial study further. In particular, researchers have shown that a model of just slightly greater complexity accounts naturally for the entire distribution of wealth, rather than just the rich end. See Nicola Scafetta, Bruce West, and Sergio Picozzi, "A trade-investment model for distribution of wealth," *Physica D* 193 (2004): 338–52.

12. In numbers, this means that each time you double the amount of water drained, you find that the number of such streams falls by a factor of about 2.7. If there are one hundred streams draining a thousand square kilometers, then there will be only about thirty-seven draining two thousand square kilometers, and so on. See Ignacio Rodriguez-Iturbe and Andrea Rinaldo, *Fractal River Basins* (Cambridge: Cambridge University Press, 1997).

13. I've written in earlier books about the widespread occurrence of power-law patterns in the natural world. See *Ubiquity* (London: Weidenfeld & Nicolson, 2000) and *Nexus* (New York: W. W. Norton, 2002).

14. G. Caldarelli et al., *European Physical Journal B* 38 (2004): 387–91.

15. See Hal Varian, "In the debate over tax policy, the power of luck shouldn't be overlooked," *New York Times*, May 3, 2001.

16. Robert Axtell, "Zipf Distribution of U.S. Firm Sizes," *Science* 293 (2001): 1818–20.

17. This was originally discovered by an economist working

with a team of physicists. See Michael Stanley et al., "Scaling Behavior in the Growth of Companies," *Nature* 379 (1996): 804–6.

18. The third pillar of the unrealistic edifice of conventional economics is the notion of equilibrium. If economic theory takes individuals to be unerringly rational and greedy, it also holds that economic outcomes at the collective level always reflect a balance among all the various forces that are acting. The standard recipe in economic theorizing is to make assumptions about what the various players in some situation seek, then work out how the interplay of their often conflicting aims will lead, through some kind of market mechanism, to some end result, a static "equilibrium." Economists seek to understand and characterize this equilibrium. Unfortunately, this rather limiting perspective effectively banishes from economic thought the consideration of change and evolution, of the dynamics of how a system gets to equilibrium. Worse yet, many researchers overlook that economic analyses assume from the outset that there has to be an equilibrium, which makes such analyses totally incapable of understanding any situation where activity does not settle down, where the forces never come to rest and balance, but continue evolving and creating perpetual novelty. This is perhaps the key reason why the market models based around Brian Arthur's El Farol bar game have proven so effective in describing real markets. They provide a natural "out of equilibrium" model, whereas orthodox economics insists on trying to force the workings of real markets into an equilibrium framework.

19. Robert Axtell, "The Emergence of Firms in a Population of Agents," Technical Report CSED, Working Paper No. 3 (Brookings Institution, 2001).

Chapter 9: FORWARD TO THE PAST

1. This example is discussed by Rob Norton in an essay available online at http://www.econlib.org/library/Enc/Unintended Consequences.html.

2. Robert K. Merton, "The Unanticipated Consequences of Purposive Social Action," *American Sociological Review* 1, no. 6 (December 1936): 894–904.

3. Alex Marshall, "Crash and Burn," *Salon,* April 16, 2005. Available online at http://dir.salon.com/story/opinion/ feature/2005/04/16/airline_woes/print.htm.

4. David Hume, *An Enquiry Concerning Human Understanding* (Boston: P. F. Collier & Son, 1910), originally published in 1748.

5. Jerry Muller, *Adam Smith in His Time and Ours* (Princeton: Princeton University Press, 1995).

6. Numerous studies show that wealth inequality all over the world has grown significantly since the early 1980s, in developing countries such as Argentina, China, Pakistan, and South Africa as well as in industrialized ones such as Australia, Finland, Britain, and the United States. In the United States, according to a detailed study by economist Edward Wolff of New York University, wealth inequality fell slowly from 1929 all the way through the mid-1970s. Since then, it has almost doubled. The richest 1 percent of families have doubled their income in this time, while the poorest 10 percent of American families now have a standard of living lower than a generation ago. In 1998, according to the most recent Federal Reserve Board Survey of Consumer Finances, the richest 1 percent of households owned 38 percent of all wealth, and the top 5 percent own more than half of all wealth. The im-

balance is, in fact, greater than in any other advanced industrial country.

7. Giovanni Cornia and Julius Court, "Inequality, Growth and Poverty in the Era of Liberalization and Globalization" (World Institute for Development Economics Research, 2001).

8. John Gray, *Straw Dogs* (London: Granta, 2002).

9. Peter Turchin, *War & Peace & War* (New York: Pi Press, 2005).

10. Edward Glaeser, Jose Scheinkman, and Andrei Shleifer, "The Injustice of Inequality," *Journal of Monetary Economics* 50 (2003): 199–222.

11. Robert Laughlin, *A Different Universe* (New York: Basic Books, 2005).

12. Sam Harris, *The End of Faith* (New York: W. W. Norton, 2004).

INDEX

NOTE: An "*n*" after the page number indicates an endnote.

objectivity, describing human events
and, 34
options trading, 65–71
Ormerod, Paul, 211n7
Oxford University, 81

Palmer, Richard, 77–79
Pareto, Vilfredo, 168–69
Pareto's natural law of wealth, 196
Paris riots (October 2005), 92, 100
patterns and natural laws
bell curve versus power law, 68–72,
213n4, 214n5
distribution of wealth, 166, 168–69
of fluid dynamics, 26–27
of genocidal events, 158–60
gravity and motion, 25–27
in history, 195–97
humans as part of nature and, 40–42
lawlike, in nonequilibrium systems,
177
magnetic fields and atoms, 104–6,
161–63, 226n10
number of participants and, 83–86
overview, 19–20
Pareto's natural law of wealth, 196
people in crowds, 6–7
phantom traffic jams, 6, 7
of rivers, 174–76, 177–78, 228n12
search for lawlike patterns, 30–32
as source of complexity, 19
thinking in, 5–10
torturing prisoners, 7–8
understanding simplicity due to,
26–27
utilizing for decision making, 73–76
wealth distribution in nature,
175–77
See also power law patterns; self-
organization
Pauli, Wolfgang, 37
peer pressure, 107
penguins, 96–97
people in crowds, 6–7, 14–15, 16
phantom traffic jams, 6, 7
phase transitions, 83–86, 162
philosophers, 29–30, 32, 33–34, 157
physics
approximations and simplification in,
161

of atoms and magnetic fields, 104–6,
161–63, 226n10
collective organization in, 10–13, 199
of copper as conductor of electricity,
109–10
destructive force of organized
molecules, 158–59
identical electrons in, 37, 42
interdependence of humans versus, 93
mathematical laws, 25–26, 168–69,
175–76, 185, 186, 228n12
and nonequilibrium systems, 177
patterns in, 26–27
phase transition in, 83, 162
quantum theory, 162–63
scope of, 41
theory acceptance in, 86
See also patterns and natural laws;
power law patterns
planetary motion, 24–26, 80, 208n3
politics, 156, 157–59, 166, 196. See also
ethnic hatred
Polyani, Karl, 217n3
Popper, Karl, 38–39
population dynamics study, 44–45
possibilities, number of participants and
coverage of, 83–86
Postmodernism Generator, 207–208n8
postmodernist social science, 18–19, 35,
207n8
Power, Samantha, 140–41, 224n1
power-hungry leaders versus social
forces, 157
power law patterns
and distribution of wealth, 168–69
effect of cheating, 183–84
for explaining adaptive systems,
185–86
fat-tail puzzle, 71–72, 78–79, 86
growth rates of firms, 180–81
Mandelbrot's discovery of, 69–72
for river networks, 175–77
predictions
as engine of science, 184–85
explanations after the fact versus,
27–28
of financial future, 81–86, 170, 216n17
of group behavior, 101–2
knowledge versus, 38–39
mechanistic, 184

A NOTE ON THE AUTHOR

MARK BUCHANAN is a physicist and science writer. He has been an editor at *Nature* and *New Scientist*, and is the author of numerous magazine and newspaper articles in the United States and the UK. Buchanan writes a column on physics for *Nature Physics*, and is also the author of two prize-nominated books, *Ubiquity: Why Catastrophes Happen* and *Nexus: Small Worlds and the Groundbreaking Theory of Networks*. He lives in Cambridgeshire, England.